"I love this book. It's an honest, refreshing look at the seasons in life when we wonder where God is. Allison reminds us that even when the ground feels dry, God is on the move."

Sheila Walsh, cohost of *LIFE Today* and author of *It's Okay Not to Be Okay*

"I just love Allison Allen! She has a heart of gold and a deep spiritual well. She's crafted a beautiful work here. Allison's message speaks to the countless women who feel dry and parched, worn out and weary from a long, arduous journey. If you need a friend to encourage you onward, if you thirst for honest and divine insights for navigating this dry season, you've come to the right place. Soak in every word. You'll be refreshed and encouraged in the process."

Susie Larson, radio host, bestselling author, national speaker

"In my experience, the 'veil gets thinner' during desert seasons, allowing us to see God more clearly. My dear friend Allison expounds on that theme so beautifully in *Thirsty for More* that you may just find yourself longing for a little more sand in your life!"

Lisa Harper, bestselling author and Bible teacher

"I love anything Allison Allen says, writes, or performs. This former Broadway actor delighted my heart and mind as we worked together in Women of Faith conferences. Her new book *Thirsty for More* speaks gently and encouragingly to those whose lives feel more like a scorching desert than a bubbling mountain stream. As Allison shares some of her own desert-like experiences, the reader feels understood and even hopeful that the desert way may well be the best water source for a parched soul."

Marilyn Meberg, author and speaker

"I wished someone had given me this book years ago when I was about to walk through the driest season of my life. I couldn't see my destiny and I certainly couldn't see any blessings coming from my pain. *Thirsty for More* is a pivotal book for every one of us to dive into. It offers so much hope whether you're in a desert or about to walk through one. Allison has such a powerful way of equipping us for such a journey and pointing us to the One who not only transforms a surrendered heart but uncovers the richest of blessings through it all. You are not alone and your destiny awaits you on the other side of your desert."

Tammy Trent, singer, songwriter,
author of *Learning to Breathe Again*

"*Thirsty for More* is a powerful read from beginning to end. Allen walks us through our desert seasons with spiritual depth, raw authenticity, and encouragement to persevere in the hard seasons. After reading, I feel more confident that my joy in being a 'Desert Daughter' is an invitation for a closer intimacy with our Father. Journeying the unknown path of trust reveals a hope perspective and the tenacity to journey on, even if we're scared. *Thirsty for More* is like having a conversation with a dear friend; a refreshing, permission-giving read of honesty, Jesus, and *more*."

Bekah Jane Pogue, author of *Choosing REAL*,
speaker, founder of Pasture

"For those who feel trapped in the fear of *not enough*, Allison Allen's *Thirsty for More* is a refreshing reminder of the hope we have when we trust God as our ultimate Provider."

Constance Rhodes, founder and CEO, FINDING*balance*, Inc.;
author of *Life Inside the "Thin" Cage*

"Allison Allen's writing is a gift. Her ability to paint pictures with words had me standing next to her in every moment as she walked me through her wilderness. She beautifully shows that the desolate and forsaken place each of us claw and scratch against going into isn't as barren as we think. Drawing parallels between today's world and Scripture, Allison reveals how we are allured by our Father into the desert. Highlighting how he can use every moment to reveal himself and refine our hearts. This book allowed me to both see the despair yet experience the hope of life's wilderness."

Jo Dee Messina, Grammy-nominated country music artist

"This book is profound. Allison reminds us that we are not alone in times of drought. Her perspective on the valleys of our lives helped me see that tough times are an opportunity that should not be wasted. This is a must-read."

Shelene Bryan, author of *Love Skip Jump*, founder of Skip1.org

"What a timely word in a day and age where the world tells us to do what makes us the happiest and to choose the easiest road possible. But we know that is not what our Savior did for us. Even though hardship is guaranteed, he promises that he will be in the midst of it with us. Allison has written a very needed and encouraging word. I guarantee whether or not you are in a desert place, you will be deeply blessed by this. We have oftentimes, as painful as it is, learned the most valuable things in the darkest of places. I pray that you would come to a more beautiful understanding about the depths of God's love for you as you read through the pages of this book."

Jeremy and Adrienne Camp, Christian recording artists

"As children of the Most High God, we live for the closeness we get to experience with our Father, for the promises he makes us. But I, like all believers do, have found myself standing on the dry, cracked clay of a desert floor, in the midst of a barren land, calling out his name, unsure of where he was. I know in my heart the truth that the presence of the Lord is always near, but Allison Allen transformed this truth into revelation for me through *Thirsty for More*. She does a beautiful job of reminding the heart that we enter the desert because we've sought and have been sought after, because God can show us his true heart for us in the vast expanse of no distractions. Thank you, Allison, for reminding me that the desert is a place of hope and not despair!"

Melissa Reeves, Emmy-nominated actress, *Days of Our Lives*

"I love, love, love this book! The desert is a lonely place, if you feel like you're walking alone or can't see God's footprints in the dry, sandy soil. And if not careful, we can get stuck there, far longer than God ever intended us to. And if we plant the wrong seeds in the desert, we may taste their bitter fruit for a very long time. Meet your new GPS in to the land of milk and honey! Her name is Allison and her words in *Thirsty for More* are like water to a parched, dry mouth. She'll give you eyes to see the beauty that's all around you, and she will hold your hand, all the way through to the other side!"

Michele Pillar, speaker, singer, creator of
The Clothesline Women's Conference, and
author of *Untangled: The Truth Will Set You Free*

"Each follower of Jesus will have times of wandering through seemingly endless desert places, and yet as Allison so clearly and passionately details, these are not times of little value. Allison communicates with a passion, experience, and wisdom that can only come through having navigated her own personal deserts. If we are open, beyond the print can be found the Truth and Presence of God—strength, blessing, companionship, and an assured hope for the path ahead."

Pastor Steve Berger, Grace Chapel, Leiper's Fork, TN

"My dear friend Allison has a way with words. Whether you're reading or listening aloud, her words capture the heart and lead one forward, pulling, tugging, encouraging onward until the heart is free. Allison teaches us that in the dry desert places, God is doing a deeper work. Don't rush the process! Moving forward may just mean remaining still for a time."

Sarah Berger, Grace Chapel, Leiper's Fork, TN

"Every one of us has our own personal seasons where we search for God in the void of life's circumstances. Allison invites us to plop down beside her as she reveals her own desert journey and how through its dry vast emptiness she found the quenching rivers of our heavenly Father. Through Allison's genuine transparency, we learn we are connected through the very fabric of our painful paths to those of our biblical ancestors to find healing and profound love in an ever-present God. Her story is overflowing with hope, and reveals to us that even the most beautiful flowers can bloom in the desert."

Shannon DeGarmo, speaker, author of *The Bounce Back Woman*, featured contributor of *Keep the Faith Radio*

"Reading Allison Allen's prose is like listening to Mozart or Beethoven. Each finely tuned word leads us in and around dry, arid deserts then brings us out into lush valleys. *Thirsty for More* leaves us thirsty for more of Allison's wisdom, insight, and strength. I am astounded by her God-given talent and will be recommending this book for years to come."

Lisa Patton, bestselling author of *Whistlin' Dixie in a Nor'easter* and *Rush*

thirsty
for
MORE

Also by Allison Allen

Shine: Stepping into the Role You Were Made For

thirsty for MORE

DISCOVERING GOD'S
UNEXPECTED BLESSINGS
IN A DESERT SEASON

Allison Allen

Revell

a division of Baker Publishing Group
Grand Rapids, Michigan

© 2018 by Storyboard, LLC

Published by Revell
a division of Baker Publishing Group
PO Box 6287, Grand Rapids, MI 49516-6287
www.revellbooks.com

Printed in the United States of America

Library of Congress Cataloging-in-Publication Data
Names: Allen, Allison (Bible Teacher), author.
Title: Thirsty for more : discovering God's unexpected blessings in a desert season / Allison Allen.
Description: Grand Rapids : Revell-Baker Publishing Group, 2018. | Includes bibliographical references and index.
Identifiers: LCCN 2018008554 | ISBN 9780800728205 (pbk. : alk. paper)
Subjects: LCSH: Christian women—Religious life. | Spirituality—Christianity. | Spiritual life—Christianity. | Deserts—Religious aspects—Christianity.
Classification: LCC BV4527 .A4383 2018 | DDC 248.8/43—dc23
LC record available at https://lccn.loc.gov/2018008554

The author is represented by Alive Literary Agency, 7680 Goddard Street, Suite 200, Colorado Springs, CO 80920, www.aliveliterary.com.

19 20 21 22 23 24   7 6 5 4 3 2

To all Desert Daughters

The desert and the parched land will be glad;
the wilderness will rejoice and blossom.

Isaiah 35:1

Contents

From One Desert Daughter
to Another

Friend,

I wonder if you find yourself in a dry season right now.

Certainly, I've been there a time or ten. Often, we cannot identify the root reasons for our dryness or even conjure up any kind of remedy. We just scan the horizon for fattened clouds—hoping the rain comes to soften the compacted soil of our circumstances, to penetrate the hard, dry hull of our hearts. Mostly, we ache for the drought to end. During the past six years, I have had the honor of talking about the desert experience, and I can recall furrowed faces and painfully raised hands, acknowledging that the wasteland was the arduous dwelling place of so many hearts.

Any way you grit it out, the spiritual desert is a difficult piece of work.

Dry, disorienting, and difficult, desert seasons have a way of spinning our hearts like little else. When our spiritual terrain is as dry and as desolate as the Sahara, when tangible evidence of God's presence slips through our fingers like sand, when loneliness dots our landscapes like tumbleweeds, we can be fairly certain we've entered a desert season. We are tempted to wonder if we have been forgotten or, worse, forsaken. For some, simply add an "ed" to the word *desert*, and you have the perfect description of how the whole experience feels emotionally. *Deserted.* And though this is not actually true, it can feel true emotionally.

If anything in your spiritual life currently resembles the desert, my heart goes out to you. The spiritual desert is not a place any of us hope to visit for any extended amount of time. Never—not once—in my entire spiritual sojourn have I petitioned God to take me on a road trip into the desert. If anything, I've asked God if I could autobahn the whole experience, flying by at whirligig speed, waving out the window as I speed past the terrifying terrain.

But the truth is that most of us don't get the drive-by desert experience. We get the land-and-linger version. Like the physical deserts of the earth, spiritual deserts are vast and large. There is no fast-forward button on them. They last as long as they last, just as they did for the leading characters of our faith: Moses. The children of Israel. David. Elijah. Jesus.

Most of us will be shaped by the ministry of the spiritual desert on this side of the veil, as our forefathers' spiritual lives were shaped by physical deserts. The spiritual desert can be a place of deep formation and even transformation, if we let it. Development often comes through difficulty. God's great narrative shouts this truth in Romans: "There's more to come! We continue to shout our praise even when we're hemmed in with troubles, because we know how troubles can develop passionate patience in us, and how that patience in turn forges

14

the tempered steel of virtue, keeping us alert for whatever God will do next" (Rom. 5:3–5 Message). Little in my life has made me feel as hemmed in as the desert experience, but precious little has produced more spiritual fruit. Or more blessing.

So what gets us through? When evidence of God's goodness feels scant and loneliness seeps into the very stuff of us, what sustains us? How do we navigate? What helps us weather such withering terrain? Where are the hidden wellsprings?

Perhaps we gain perspective by peeling back the layers of the experience as a whole. Perhaps we are sustained by allowing the original desert walker, Jesus, to reframe the sandy sojourn for us in unique ways. Perhaps we allow ourselves to acknowledge that we thirst for more than just physical bread and water. Perhaps we navigate the dry season by mining the redemptive desert experiences of Scripture, finding that the desert, in God's hands, always reveals hidden bounty, blessing, and beauty.

Desert daughter, let's dig deep for those hidden blessings. Let's thirst for more and find our cup running over.

Let's discover that in Christ, even the desert blooms.

With undying hope,
Allison

A Desert Walker's Wellspring

Therefore I am now going to allure her;
    I will lead her into the desert
    and speak tenderly[1] to her.
There I will give her back her vineyards,
    and will make the Valley of Achor[2] a door of hope.
There she will sing[3] as in the days of her youth,
    as in the day she came up out of Egypt.
"In that day," declares the LORD,
    "you will call me 'my husband';
    you will no longer call me 'my master.'
I will remove the names of the Baals from her lips;
    no longer will their names be invoked.
In that day I will make a covenant for them
    with the beasts of the field and the birds of the air
    and the creatures that move along the ground.
Bow and sword and battle
    I will abolish from the land,
    so that all may lie down in safety.
I will betroth you to me forever;
    I will betroth you in righteousness and justice,
    in love and compassion.
I will betroth you in faithfulness,
    and you will acknowledge the LORD."

. . . .

HOSEA 2:14–20 OXFORD NIV

1

Spiritual Deserts
and Leather Couches

Therefore I am now going to allure her;
I will lead her into the desert
and speak tenderly to her.

Hosea 2:14 Oxford NIV

One day when I was sitting in my cell, my thoughts were
troubling me, suggesting that I should go to the desert
and see what I could see there.

Marcarius the Great, desert father[1]

Desert Dwellers

In early Christendom, men and women, called the desert fathers and mothers, moved into the deserts of Syria, Egypt, and

the surrounding areas to seek God and to remove themselves from the impurities of the world. They truly wanted to get away from it all, and for them, that meant moving into the desert and making their address those desert caves.

For many of these radical followers, the church, newly instated as the religion of the realm, oozed corruption. Writer Keith Beasley-Topliffe put it this way: "Some may have become disgusted with the secularization of Christianity, believing that it had become too easy to be a Christian."[2] An institutionalized church made following Jesus easy. Too easy. To the desert crew, the more austere spiritual disciplines were not easily practiced in a society in which following Jesus had become the religious soup du jour. The cross had lost its cost. Self-denial was a suggestion, not a way of life. So they headed for the desert, where the harsh elements would truly make life costly, physically and spiritually.

They were thirsty for more.

The daily lives of the desert fathers and mothers were marked by austerity, poverty, and intentional solitude. The desert fathers and mothers were the progenitors of the monastic movements—think convents and monasteries.

These desert dwellers became known for their intense dedication to the faith, and multitudes caravanned into the desert to hear their wisdom, which was collected into what is now known as the desert sayings. Many of the sayings are supremely insightful; others near inscrutable. Sometimes desert communities sprang up around these desert occupants, their solitary way of life attracting, rather than repelling, followers.[3]

The desert fathers and mothers intrigue me, even though for many years I knew little of them. Just that name—desert fathers and mothers—sounded so . . . distinguished. So *other*. In my Protestant upbringing, they were never mentioned. Only as I began writing for another project did I discover a bit more about them. To me, uncovering these radical men and women, hidden out there in the desert sand, pioneers of the desert experience, was like discovering some unknown branches of the family tree—a hidden treasure in one's own backyard. Unexpected treasures.

We could go on and on about their contributions, but the intriguing fact I most want to focus on concerning this fantastically oddball crew is that they chose the desert of their own free will. They *chose* the desert. They abandoned every material possession they had ever called their own and moved "on up" to the desert.

We spend so much time running from the spiritual desert, while these brave souls ran to it—spiritually and geographically—understanding that venturing into hostile surroundings causes the most vivid desert roses to bloom beautifully in the soul. Understanding that the same desert wind that pelts the skin with sand gives the bird its flight. Understanding that desert fruit is richer simply because of the battle it must fight to grow in such inhospitable elements.

Even with the guidance of these weathered and wrinkled guides, I would rarely, if ever, choose the desert. I would go so far as to say that I have been a desert hater. I'd rather climb Everest ice with Jesus than sit with him in Negev sand. I'm not going willingly. All too often, I find myself resembling the nation of Israel, of which God said in Hosea, "Therefore I am now going to *allure* her; I will lead her into the desert and speak tenderly to her" (2:14 Oxford NIV, emphasis added).

That word *allure* is interesting. It is not used much in Scripture, and when it is used, such as in Hosea, the word's meaning is similar to what it means in modern times. The word

21

translated as "allure" is from the Hebrew word *paw-thaw*, and it means "to make open to, to persuade, to entice, and even to seduce."[4] To my mind, it is as if God was dangling a holy carrot in front of the nation of Israel so that they might follow him into the desert (or wilderness, depending on your translation)—a place to which no right-thinking person or nation would really want to go. (For future reference, one of the definitions of the word translated "wilderness" in your Bible version is "desert," and, my goodness, isn't that apropos?) Every desert experience I have ever weathered has felt wild and unpredictable and never would have been a place I would have gone unless allured.

And in 2011, something just like that happened.

The Ultimate Holy Carrot

This story began as stories are wont to do, innocuously enough, around March in the year of our Lord 2011. I was preparing to go to Ohio for an event. However, the strangest thing kept happening. I would stand to work on my teaching only to be stonewalled by a wave of nausea.

With my background in acting, I knew what it meant to work "through it." Sore throat? Sore ankles? Bring 'em on. But being on the edge of losing your cookies all day long? Take it away. Please, take it away. I made an appointment posthaste with my primary doctor to see if I could get some miracle drug to knock back the nausea to a pesky, manageable nuisance so I could do the event. Appointment duly made for the next day, I went to sleep.

But as sleep and I have always had a complicated relationship, I found myself wide awake at about 2:00 a.m. It was in the dark hour that a brilliant idea pinged me: I remembered that I had tons of pregnancy sticks squirreled away in my bathroom drawer and that nausea was sometimes a symptom of pregnancy. (My astute medical insight stuns me even to this day!)

I knew immediately what I should do: I should take advantage of the pregnancy stick prepper I had become. Allow me to explain.

Several years prior, I had performed a one-woman drama in which the character reached her cathartic moment when she realized she was pregnant and could not pass on a legacy of self-hatred to her child. Because that realization was triggered by a physical prop—a pregnancy stick—I had been plagued by the actor's nightmare of reaching into my back pocket at that moment in the play only to be "stickless." Therefore, I carried copious bundles of unused pregnancy sticks with me every time I went on the road to perform the one-woman drama. Many of them were still residing in my bathroom drawer years later on the nauseating night in question.

So I thought, *Why not? There's not a snowball's chance I'm preggo, but why not? Might as well put those pregnancy sticks to their intended use.* So I did due diligence, and there, underneath the dim bathroom lights, I saw it. The reason. The culprit. The best news in all the whole wide world for someone like me.

A positive sign. The faintest pink bloom of hope.

Immediately, I talked myself out of pregnancy as the reason for the nausea, thinking there must be some cosmic mistake. I ran (carefully, now, due to the outrageous possibility) to my computer to research false positives on pregnancy tests. My memory served me correctly, though, as Doctor Google confirmed: a person might experience false negatives, but only very, very rarely will one receive a false positive. It turns out that—in most cases—there really is no such thing as being a little bit pregnant.

I said exactly nada to Jonathan, who blissfully slept through the whole Lucille Ball physical comedy routine unfolding in our house that night as I careened up and down stairs to consult Google and ran back into the bathroom to see if the plus was really a plus or just wishful addition.

Not only had I just celebrated the second anniversary of my thirty-ninth birthday, which made me a little mature to be cooking a croissant in the oven, but Jonathan and I had also struggled with what is commonly called secondary infertility for years, making the miracle all the more unlikely.

We had encountered no problem getting pregnant with our first baby, Levi, who by the time of this story was eight. But we had run into years of misses with having a second child. Once, near the end of the seven-year sojourn of secondary infertility, I had sought hormones to help my stubborn, nonfruitful body produce life. In that encounter, I had learned that even magic medicine would only make me produce more aged eggs; it would do nothing about the quality of the eggs. My eggs were officially old. Thank you, archaic eggs.

All that to say, I had no desire to create false hope or false freak-out in my husband in the middle of the night. *Holy diaper bill. We'll be leaning into sixty when this baby graduates from high school. Do normal people spring for college and retirement at the same time?* I went back to bed and tried to catch at least one z. The next morning I rolled into my doc's office, rocking that pregnancy stick in my back pocket. Oh, honey, yes, one does not give up the evidence, especially when one is officially "advanced maternal age."

I said to the nurse, producing the stick as I did so, "Have you ever seen one of these be wrong?" (My dramatic side was peeking through the curtain, I admit.) She gave a wry smile and carefully said that, personally, she had not. The staff promptly had me perform due diligence again and wait—right there—for the results. Finally, my doctor came in and produced some mash-up of these words: "Well, my dear. You're not sick with the flu. You are sick with child."

So we experienced what we truly believe was a miracle. Ironically, about a week prior to the unexpected news, we had given away every stick of baby furniture that we had been saving "just in case." They always say that if you want to get pregnant, buy a dog. I say give away all that baby furniture moldering in the garage. I recall standing in that garage, like at an altar, surrender and sadness mingling, thinking, "Oh, Lord, if an only child is what you have chosen for us, we accept it. Isaac, the only son of Abraham and Sarah, was pretty important in the scheme of things. A patriarch *and* an only child. And anyway, you're not limited by quantity. We accept your will." Little did I know in that moment of surrender that a miracle was already growing in my belly. In some ways, I believe that the moment we surrender, some kind of creative miracle is already gestating.

As the miraculous, new reality sank in, we made giddy phone calls. We experienced quizzical and kind looks as we told people we were pregnant. We even knew the names: Maggie, if a girl, and Luke, if a boy. Our older son's proclivity for all things Star Wars may or may not have had something to do with the namesake Luke. We told Levi we had to draw the line at Skywalker as a middle name, much to his chagrin.

Around twenty weeks, just after we had discovered the baby's gender (ready those lightsabers, people!), we had quite a scare. I went in for a routine ultrasound and during the procedure,

I saw a terrified look fly across the face of the young tech, who hadn't yet developed a poker face when seeing disturbing results. I asked her what was up, and what I remember distinctly is that she didn't answer me. I followed her gaze to a set of numbers that were appearing on a giant screen, to a particular numerical set that seemed to be the source of her furrowed brow. The number was changing: 1.2, 0.8, 1.1, 0.9. I asked what the numbers represented as the number finally came to rest at 1.2. She replied that the numbers were the length of my cervix. I asked her what the number should be at twenty weeks, and she replied, "About 3.0 to 4.0."

I remember thinking *not good.* At twenty weeks, with only 1.2 centimeters of cervix left, I was in trouble. Simply put, the pregnancy structure wasn't holding, and at twenty weeks (and forty-one years old), that was a major problem. I had what is medically referred to as an incompetent cervix. (Don't get me started on that name. My poor cervix never failed any standardized test that I am aware of.)

What I remember next was being asked to lie very still as the center's head physician confirmed the findings. Then I remember a cacophony outside the door as Jonathan rushed in, leaving our son, Levi, outside in the hall. There were whispered phone calls that I couldn't quite make out and a rising terror in my throat. Plans were being made for me to go directly across the street to the hospital for admittance. Once there, we discovered our limited options: I was unlikely to get pregnant again if we lost the baby, so "wait and see" was a huge roll of the proverbial dice. A surgery, called a cervical cerclage, would be our best (and likely only) shot. We quickly learned that the risks of the surgery were great and that there was a strong possibility the structure

26

itself would be punctured during the procedure, causing immediate birth.

I didn't realize I was crying until I tasted the salt. I remember naively saying, "He would be a preemie, wouldn't he?"

A sober medical professional delivered the difficult news. "No, Allison, he won't be a preemie. At twenty weeks, likely he won't be viable. I'm so sorry."

To Jonathan and me, there was no other choice but to risk. I remember experiencing what I know now was shock. My teeth chattered and my body shook as I was wheeled into the sterile operating room; the room had been plunged into a sudden winter.

I had the emergency surgery, and after the surgery, we were told that I would be embarking on bed rest—bed rest that would last for three solid months. *Three solid months.* This was the very definition of torment—scratch that, a tormenting desert—for a type A sister like me. But make no mistake, I would have sat on my leather couch for the "whole nine" if doing so meant saving Luke.

Bed rest went a little something like this: one walk downstairs in the morning *to the couch,* where I would remain *on the couch*—until I was allowed one walk up the stairs at the end of the day. Getting a glass of water was out. Prepping a meal—prepping a nursery? All out. I could use the bathroom under my own auspices, I am happy to report. But quickly, mind you. In addition, I could partake of a shower once every three days for a grand total of three minutes. I was allowed to venture outside the house once a week for a myriad of specialists' appointments. I admit it—I looked forward to that day as much as a teenager does the day the license is valid and the braces come off.

Other than that, it was largely me, myself, and I on that couch—a leather couch that felt an awful lot like a spiritual desert.

Now, I want to make something clear: our church and our friends stepped up incredibly. They circled the proverbial wagons and bore our burdens. Meals. Visits. Cleaning. Carting around our older son. Books to read. Et cetera and et cetera multiplied infinitely by et cetera. At the time, we had no blood family where we lived, so the body of Christ became our family in ways we never could have envisioned. My family and I are eternally grateful for the care and "carrying" we received.

But even the incredible outpouring couldn't do the one thing that I thought I wanted more than anything else: it couldn't fill up all the hours I spent alone. Folks stopped by for visits (which I treasured above gold), but you can do the math, right? Loads of solitary hours were still left in a day. And as I have already said, I'm type A to the marrow, so the hours and hours of solitary communion with the couch—with nothing much to do but sit still—were hard and painful.

But even harder than the intense communion with the couch was the intense communion with the contents of my heart. All that unfilled, unoccupied time became a crowbar used by God to pry open my heart. Things leaked out that I had not taken time to look at. Not in a really long time.

Whenever I would get a cut as a kid, my mom, like most, would say, "Make sure to let it get some air." Letting something breathe was the first step to warding off infection, in her sage opinion.

Well, there was a lot locked in my bed-rest heart that I had never given "spiritual air." Like unexpressed expectations—sometimes of people, sometimes of God. Like qualities that confounded me about God himself. Like traces of unforgiveness.

These were all things I thought had been rooted out but were still lurking, hidden beneath the busyness. I needed to do business with God, but I hadn't stopped in so long. *Bed rest was nothing but stopping.* Physically. Emotionally. Spiritually. Bed rest functioned in me like musical rests function in music. Rests are integral to a good piece of music, but often they are rushed, and sometimes they are overlooked altogether. However, without the rests, music is not quite music; it is just a series of unending, largely indistinguishable tones. It is quiet that gives sound its meaning. I remember multiple chorus teachers through the years instructing, "Mind your rests. Mind your rests."

My desert was nothing but a forced rest. And I had no choice but to mind it.

So there I was, minding my three-month pause as God searched me and knew my heart (Ps. 139:23). There on the couch I told him the little *t* truths I was carrying around—things that were *my* truth but not *his* truth, things that were ultimately handicapping my relationship with him.

I spat the poison out and found that he could more than handle it. He was patient. He was kind. But he was unrelenting. Something about the intensity of the desert experience brought all my dross to the surface. Once it was all out in the open (or on the sofa, as the case may be), he gave some very specific instructions.

Surrender. Let go. These old things don't serve you anymore. This desert, daughter, is for your surrender, and surrender is the doorway to a new spiritual season. It's time to wave the flag.

Somehow, with the incredible grace of Christ poured out on the girl on the couch, I was enabled to do just that. For the first time in my life, I was able to recline into the Isaiah passage that says, "In repentance and rest is your salvation" (30:15), rather than just recite it. Bed rest forced me to surrender to rest and repentance.

In case I ever forget the spiritual fruit of my "surrender season" on the couch, God gave me some physical fruit of surrendering to the desert as a holy reminder. God allured my heart to a desert place that he might speak tenderly to me, just as he did the wayward nation of Israel. I don't know that I would have willingly followed him into "a dry and weary land" (Ps. 63:1 ESV).

But God dangled a holy carrot—one that could not be resisted—and I followed into a land of unexpected blessing.

Like the desert fathers and mothers who willingly followed God "into the desert, into a land that couldn't be farmed" (Jer. 2:2 GW), I want to remain a "desert daughter" who also says yes to whatever season—desert or otherwise—God has for me. I want to believe to the marrow that "the LORD will comfort Zion; he will comfort all her waste places, he will make her wilderness like Eden, and her desert like the garden of the LORD" (Isa. 51:3 CSB).

Reflections

One day when I was sitting in my cell, my thoughts were troubling me, suggesting that I should go to the desert and see what I could see there.

Marcarius the Great, desert father[5]

Keep close to Jesus.

Paul, desert father[6]

I know the difficulty of a desert season. Feeling marooned. Feeling lonely and dry. Yet, words from the desert fathers and mothers can be a bread-crumb trail for us through the arid, trying, and character-defining experience of the desert.

Have you ever walked through a desert season? If so, how did it feel? What did your desert look like? Describe the lay of the land. Did you go willingly, hoping to catch a glimpse of God out there in the craggy land? Or were you more like ancient Israel—allured by God into a place that, given the choice, you would not want to go?

If you are in a desert right now, ask Jesus what there is to see there spiritually. And, above all, ask God how you might keep close to him as you journey through the desert terrain.

2

Desert Whats and Whys

Witness the dark night of the soul in individual saints.

Flannery O'Connor[1]

A brother . . . asked Abba Bessarion, "What should I do?"
The old man replied, "Keep silence and not compare
yourself with others."

The Sayings of the Desert Fathers[2]

Desert Whats

She was the picture of put together and as lovely inside as out.
To me, she'd been a generous and giving force in our church
body, possessing such shine, so I was a little surprised when I
happened upon her crying in the bathroom. (Who else thinks

that the most paradigm-shifting encounters in church happen in the bathroom?)

She had just attended a class I had taught on the desert experience, so I approached timidly, wondering if her tears flowed from a place of desert dryness.

"You okay?" I asked.

She shook her head tenderly, decidedly, and answered me with some form of these words: "I can't get a job, Allison. Nothing works. I've been on more interviews than I can shake a stick at. I can't even pick up a seasonal retail job. What is wrong with me?"

I looked at this accomplished woman who had, for years, assisted entertainment moguls at the highest levels, this lover of God who had humbly pursued any and every job opportunity that had come her way only to be met with an unending echo of no.

She looked at me and added, "I'm in a desert of unemployment."

My dear sister, whose experience I share with permission, was in a desert in this one area of her life. In other areas of her life, she was experiencing blessing, but running alongside those rivers of blessing was the desolate bank of a desert.

Some of us could say amen right alongside my friend, couldn't we? In many areas of our lives, we are experiencing a cornucopia of goodness and grace, and yet in one tender area, there seems to be a persistent, unmitigated dryness and difficulty, even dearth. I've known women who were in a desert in their marriage or in friendship or even in regards to their purpose in God's kingdom.

Other desert residents are living through what is commonly referred to as a "dark night of the soul" (we get the phrase from the title of St. John of the Cross's epic poem dealing with all things trying and triumphant, *Noche Oscura Del Alma*). In this dark-night-of-the-soul season, all seems gutted, the felt presence of God agonizingly absent. Mother Teresa experienced something akin to this type of dark desert for years upon years, according to those who knew her best.[3] One of the oddest and most memorable happenings of my life occurred as I stood in a line after the blessing of a convent in the DC area dedicated to caring for society's least and last—a blessing which Mother Teresa presided over. Invited by a dear friend, I could never have imagined that I would wind up being prayed for by her. (Everyone in the line was.) Like many who ever saw her in person, I saw her as a bright flame: joyful and passionate and on a silver-bullet mission from heaven. Yet this spiritual oasis to so many often dwelled in a spiritual desert. Her missives tell the hard tale: "The silence and the emptiness is so great—that I look and do not see—Listen and do not hear."[4] One can almost imagine the lament of Psalm 44:24—"Why do you hide your face?"—lacing through such searing letters.

The desert fathers and mothers gave the overarching emptiness the name *acedia*.[5] Based on the writings of the desert residents Benedicta Ward defined *acedia* in her book *The Sayings of the Desert Fathers* as "despondency, depression, listlessness, a distaste for life without any specific reason."[6] Is it possible that acedia was an early extrabiblical expression of depression? I have known many a saint whose desert walk stretched on like an acedia marathon, a relentless dark night, like Mother Teresa's.

Still others of us have had shorter desert seasons—like mine on the couch—with definite beginnings, middles, and endings, a secluded spiritual experience during which we confronted deep questions about God's presence and even care.

Some of us are in that tough emotional terrain right now, with no sense of the experience's expiration date. Our souls feel as if they have been marooned in the middle of the Sahara.

Some of us may feel we are being led into the desert even now. A stripping wind has begun to blow. A shift of direction has occurred, an unexpected turn, and the desert looms large over the horizon.

Spiritual deserts take as many different forms as physical deserts. Think of the mysterious Gobi. The vast Sahara. The do-not-run-out-of-gas Death Valley. The odd Antarctic. (Though it is icy there, little to no precipitation falls, technically making it a desert.) Our deserts can look so different from those of others, and comparing deserts is often an exercise in frustration. By nature, dry seasons are deeply personal, solitary, and oddly indefinable. Yet, no matter how the spiritual desert manifests itself, the buffeting sojourn shows us what we're made of like little else. And, I believe, no one seriously intent on being conformed into the image of Christ goes without its peculiar ministry.

We can safely say that the desert experience is going to touch our hearts, probably more than once, in varying degrees and in varying ways throughout our lives.

Desert Whys

Handling the what is always easier if we can grasp the why. At least this was the case for me. Somehow I could nestle into the desert wilderness—the what—because I began to grasp a growing sense of the why. The why gave me perseverance. The why gave me hope. And hope helped me better grasp the grace that was present the whole time.

Though there can be as many reasons for the desert as there are ways to roll sushi, Scripture contains three *whys* for the desert that we will return to over and over again in this book. I like to think of them as three pegs of my "desert tent" when I find myself in a desolate season.

Jesus uses the desert to reveal the heart.

Jesus uses the desert to restore the heart.

Jesus uses the desert to release the heart.

Quite often, the desert is all about the heart.

Reveal

Let's take the first peg. The primary thing I had to deal with on that desert couch was the unexpressed contents of my burdened and sinful heart. I hadn't stopped in so long that I had lost any real sense of what I was toting around in the center of my chest. God wanted me to see what forces were warring against my heart. He wanted heart revelation, and he used the desert to get it. Amazingly, God gives this objective as the reason for the Israelites' forty-year lollygag through the wilderness: "Remember how the LORD your God led you all the way in the wilderness these forty years, to humble and test you *in order to know what was in your heart*, whether or not you would keep his commands" (Deut. 8:2, emphasis added).

For some of us, one of the great blessings of the desert is this: God invites us into a sacred space where we can exchange our little *t* truths for his capital *T* Truth. Some of us are lugging around beliefs that we would promise to the tips of our pedicured toes are undyingly true—they feel true, they seem true, they even ring true—but when put through the trying circumstances of the desert, our little *t* truths are often unmasked as counterfeit.

My little *t* truth: I am alone in my desert.

God's capital *T* Truth: You may be lonely in your desert, but you are never alone. I will never leave you or forsake you. I am no stranger to deserts. I am right here with you.

In the desert, where our little *t* truths are unmasked, we can choose to exchange them for ultimate Truth.

There is nothing quite like the harsh desert climate to reveal what is real.

What about the other two pegs? Restore and Release? The heartbroken husband and prophet Hosea has something to say about them.

Restore

> Therefore I am now going to allure her;
> I will lead her into the desert
> and speak tenderly to her. (Hos. 2:14 Oxford NIV)

Though many versions of the Bible translate the first verse as "I will lead her into the desert and speak *tenderly* to her," other versions translate the passage this way: "I will lead her into the desert and speak *comfortably* to her." That one word took my breath away six years ago when I was preparing to teach on the desert for the first time. The translation "comfortably" more accurately hones in on an unusual meaning contained in the Hebrew word itself. The word *comfortably* comes from the Hebrew word *leb,* which is an ancient form of the word *heart.*[7] That is why Young's Literal Translation interprets the Hosea passage this way: "Therefore, lo, I am enticing her, and have caused her to go to the wilderness, and I have spoken unto her heart" (2:14). In essence, God was saying, "I'm taking Israel into the desert to have a truthful and tender talk with her heart."

The Hebrew word translated "comfortably" also contains the interesting root *al,* which means "upon, within, beside."[8] To my mind, God is saying, "I am going to speak tenderly to all of her heart—to the things that weigh upon it, to the things that reside within it, and to outside forces that run alongside it." There was no part of his people's hearts that he didn't want to hear about and speak to. God wanted to bless her heart—not in a Southern way but in a sovereign way.

How beautiful. How restorative. I can think of little in my life that has been as restorative for my heart as the uninterrupted seasons of conversation with Christ in the desert.

Release

There I will give her back her vineyards,
    and will make the Valley of Achor a door of hope.
There she will respond as in the days of her youth,
    as in the day she came up out of Egypt. (Hos. 2:15
    Oxford NIV)

Have you ever been twisted up tight over a task or a situation only to finally experience that exquisite moment when the pressure valve is released?

You've climbed the mountain. You've written the dissertation. You've unpacked the last box from the cross-country move. You've surrendered the burden to Jesus. The struggle loses its stranglehold. And then. The skies crack. Freedom flows. Hope blooms.

You've been released, my friend.

I've felt that way after many a test, and especially after many an opening night. As a performer, I have been a part of many shows, from my debut in kindergarten all the way to belting on Broadway, and know well the work and war to get a show "up." Much like with the journey to opening a show, when the spiritual journey has been arduous and focused and taken more resources than I had to give, when I can finally look at the experience and say, "God did that for my good," when the work is done and I can finally breathe to the bottom of my lungs, I know release has finally come. There is nothing else like it.

God promises us something similar in and after our desert experiences. For most of us, desert seasons are as intense as anything we have ever suffered. Daily, we must press into grace to take the next step. We also must pray for something that is none too hip in our world: endurance. There were times on that desert couch when I thought, *I cannot endure one more second with me, myself, and I and the intense business the Triune God is doing with my heart.* But God gave more enduring grace for the long trek, and he promised a bevy of blessings for my heart if I would submit to the experience. I wanted escape from my circumstances, but God wanted to release me in the midst of my circumstances.

Escaping from jail is very different from being released from jail. Escaping—at least to me—intimates still being under some type of judgment or legal bounds and hopping on the last train out of town, hoping no one is on your tail. But when

40

you are released? Fully released? Well, that is something only God can do.

I think of Paul and Silas in the Philippian jail. There they were . . . in chains, making music at midnight, interceding in their incarceration, when suddenly a great quake shook the foundations of the prison like a Southern twister. God blew the doors off. Everyone's (not just Paul's and Silas's) chains disintegrated like they were mere cobwebs. The freedom story continued on, with radical salvation coming to a previously freaked-out and near-suicidal guard and his entire family. Ultimately, Paul and Silas got to walk out of the city, with an official apology tucked in their pockets no less. Fully free. Fully released. Because God had done the releasing.

Though my desert experience was different from the dramatic and explosive story in Acts, I was still released from a jail I didn't realize I was imprisoned in. And God used the desert to do it, loading me down with blessings like fresh hope, reinvigorated worship, and restored fruitfulness when the whole experience was finally finished. Released, indeed.

In the meantime, as I began to catch a small glimmer of that incredible end, I actually started to long for the desert to complete its full work and have its full weight.

I thirsted for Jesus's desert ministry in my life and wanted every sandy blessing he sifted through his scarred hands.

Reflections

Do not always want everything to turn out as you think it should, but rather, as God pleases.

Nilus, desert father[9]

Fellow sojourner, have you ever considered that God has strenuous work—perhaps unique work—to do in your heart during your desert season? Perhaps the work might be different than you may have initially imagined. Though we will hammer each peg in as we go along, have you caught a glimpse of how God might reveal your heart, restore your heart, and release your heart through this parched passage?

3

Preparation

A house is not built by beginning at the top and working down. You must begin with the foundations in order to reach the top.

John the Dwarf, desert father[1]

Now an angel of the Lord said to Philip, "Go south to the road—the desert road—that goes down from Jerusalem to Gaza."

Acts 8:26

*W*omen, men, and ministries greatly used by God will have often come by way of the desert. I believe this to the marrow.

Behind every saint is a story, and often that story includes a chapter (or multiple chapters) of lengthy preparation in the desert. I think especially of Paul, the apostle who, after receiving a vision from heaven and speaking with Jesus himself, spent years on and off in Tarsus in Turkey making tents with Aquila and Priscilla. Paul went to see them, and because he was a tentmaker as they were, he stayed and worked with them (Acts 18:2–3). Speaking of tents, remember those tent pegs?

Revealing the heart.

Restoring the heart.

Releasing the heart.

Those pegs that we want to drive deep into the sand of our experience? Well, tent pegs require a tent—a "tent" of preparation, if you will.

Prerequisite

God often uses the harsh, desert climate like a spiritual prerequisite of sorts—much like the classes I had to take during my first two years of college. Before I could take the enviable master classes my junior and senior year would offer, I had to weather some classes that were meant to sift me—*Can you really make it to voice and speech every day at 7:50 a.m. after rehearsing until midnight?*—and prepare me—*If you can thrive under this schedule, then working in the professional world will feel like a cinch.* Man, we wanted the plum, upperclass roles and the plum, upperclass schedules, but we had to graduate from those plumb-hard prerequisites that came first.

No other way around it, only through it, even in college. Preparation precedes promotion. Difficulty precedes the desired end. The desert precedes destiny. And if the desert was deemed necessary for Jesus, we can be assured the same will be true of us.

First in the Water

Before we cannonball into this next section, I want to make sure we are all jumping into the same river: Jesus was—in all ways—fully man and fully God, blameless and without sin. Not even a hair-width's breadth of doubt about it. And yet Hebrews also says something very interesting of Christ: "Although he was a son, he learned obedience through what he suffered" (5:8 ESV).

How could the perfect, blameless, and sinless Son of God need to learn anything? Some theologians believe that this Scripture passage is speaking of Jesus's way of going through what we go through—progressing as we progress—learning obedience to our good heavenly Father as we surely must; yet unlike us, Christ did all these things without sin.[2]

In other words, he went first into every experience. And he went first perfectly. He suffered perfectly. He obeyed perfectly. He prepared perfectly. And he endured the desert perfectly. The Bible tell us this about Jesus's experience not to make us feel bad about how we journey in the desert but so that we will know that the perfect One is there with us.

In Hebrews 4:15–16, the Bible renders a beautiful picture of this truth: "For we do not have a high priest who is unable to sympathize with our weaknesses, but we have one who has been tempted in every way, just as we are—yet he did not sin. Let us then approach God's throne of grace with confidence, so that we may receive mercy and find grace to help us in our time of need." Commentators point out that the temptation referred to in verse 15 is none other than Jesus's own desert battle with the enemy[3]—a battle that he won perfectly, sinlessly. This truth gives me enduring hope: though I will never walk the desert perfectly, I have access—deep, abiding access—to the One who did. The perfect One stands as a fore guard and a rear guard as the sandstorms begin to swirl around my desert tent.

Spirit Led

Luke tells us about Jesus's sojourn in the desert and what came after. This is a lengthy portion of Scripture, but I hope you will grab a pencil and make notes as God whispers to your heart. In fact, I'm going to highlight some key phrases that jump out at me like my six-year-old does during hide-and-seek.

> Jesus returned from the Jordan *full of the Holy Spirit* and was *led by the Spirit into the desert*, where he was tempted by the Devil for forty days. In all that time he ate nothing, so that he was hungry when it was over.
>
> The Devil said to him, "If you are God's Son, order this stone to turn into bread."
>
> But Jesus answered, *"The scripture says, 'Human beings cannot live on bread alone.'"*
>
> Then the Devil took him up and showed him in a second all the kingdoms of the world. "I will give you all this power and all this wealth," the Devil told him. "It has all been handed over to me, and I can give it to anyone I choose. All this will be yours, then, if you worship me."
>
> Jesus answered, "The scripture says, 'Worship the Lord your God and serve only him!'"
>
> Then the Devil took him to Jerusalem and set him on the highest point of the Temple, and said to him, "If you are God's Son, throw yourself down from here. For the scripture says, 'God will order his angels to take good care of you.' It also says,

'They will hold you up with their hands so that not even your feet will be hurt on the stones.'"

But Jesus answered, "The scripture says, 'Do not put the Lord your God to the test.'"

When the Devil finished tempting Jesus in every way, he left him for a while.

Then Jesus returned to Galilee, *and the power of the Holy Spirit was with him. The news about him spread throughout all that territory. He taught in the synagogues and was praised by everyone.*

Then Jesus went to Nazareth, where he had been brought up, and on the Sabbath he went as usual to the synagogue. He stood up to read the Scriptures and was handed the book of the prophet Isaiah. He unrolled the scroll and found the place where it is written,

> "The Spirit of the Lord is upon me,
>   because he has chosen me to bring good news to
>   the poor.
> He has sent me to proclaim liberty to the captives
>   and recovery of sight to the blind,
> to set free the oppressed
>   and announce that the time has come
>   when the Lord will save his people."

Jesus rolled up the scroll, gave it back to the attendant, and sat down. All the people in the synagogue had their eyes fixed on him, as he said to them, "This passage of scripture has come true today, as you heard it being read." (Luke 4:1–21 GNT, emphasis added)

These true stories always upend my mind when I read them. Battles between shine and shadow. God's Truth trouncing the enemy's claptrap. The hometown son debuting as the Son of God.

But something else in the first lines of the passage upends me down to my DNA.

The Scripture passage starts off with an audacious statement about Jesus's desert experience, saying that being *full of the Holy Spirit,* he was *led by the Spirit* . . . into the desert. Every time I read this, I have to sit down with it afresh. The Holy Spirit, part of the Triune God, led Jesus into the desert.

Just prior to this, God pronounced a blessing on his Son in an audible voice from heaven (this happens only three times in the New Testament), saying, "This is my Son, whom I love; with him I am well pleased" (Matt. 3:17).

And then what comes next on the highlight reel? You guessed it—the desert.

If I were the director of Jesus's story, I would storyboard the scenes a bit differently. Close up: Jesus rising from the water as the audible blessing from God is pronounced. Cut to: Growing influence. Wide angle: Huge ministry. Close up: Speaking truth to power. Pan: Thousands and thousands coming to the knowledge of the Savior. You get the picture.

What I'm saying is that if the God of the universe speaks of you as his beloved and unique Son and declares his love for you, you might think the next step would be an immediate revival the likes of which the world has never seen. In my wildest imagination, I would never compose a screenplay in which the progression would be baptism, audible blessing . . . howling desert. But in this case, and in many cases, this is the unusual economy of God.

The desert precedes destiny.

If the desert of preparation was deemed necessary for the Author and Finisher of our faith, then, I believe, it will be deemed necessary for us. I've met women who automatically assumed they were in a desert season due to sin or rebellion, and while that can be the case (the Bible says that the rebellious dwell in a dry and weary land), it is very often *not* the case. Often, the desert is not about misdeed but about maturity.

Especially as we come face-to-face with the ifs and buts there.

If

Jesus's desert experience was unusual. He went in for a forty-day match with the enemy of his (and our) soul. And he went into it fasting—not just from food but from water as well. The average person perishes without water in three to four days.[4] The thirst must have been unbearable. But Jesus was drinking and eating supernatural provision. In this encounter, we are witnessing truly supra—above the natural—provision for Jesus's desert preparation.

There were several specific battlefronts in this desert war. On one front was the obvious battle for supremacy via the tools of humility or pride. On another was the battle over the appropriation or misappropriation of God's revealed Word. And on another was the battle over worship. Those three battles alone would be more than enough for a super-satisfying summer blockbuster.

Perhaps, though, one more desert battle was taking place, possibly larger in many ways than all the others rolled together. I've always believed that Jesus was engaging in an epic battle involving identity.

Twice in the Scripture passage, the enemy trots out a very potent phrase: "If you are the Son of God." Oh, that word *if.* As a young believer, I heard many a pastor warn about the potency of *if* in the enemy's mouth. *If* is a tricky, diminutive word with many meanings, but it often denotes uncertainty or conditionality. In Satan's first line of attack, before he gets to worship or provision or rule and reign, he attacks Jesus with the bludgeoning club of *if*. He attacks Christ's relatedness to his heavenly Father. He attacks Jesus's identity as a son. *If you are the Son of God.* Every sneaky thing Satan tries to get Jesus to do starts with *if*.

And though I cannot prove it and I want to ask Jesus about it when I get to heaven, I believe that each time the enemy slimed him with a doubt-inducing if, a certain phrase echoed in his holy mind like a remedy, a phrase that his own heavenly Father had just previously spoken of him:

> This is my Son, whom I love; with him I am well pleased. (Matt. 3:17)

Every time the enemy advanced, I wonder if Jesus thought, "I am his beloved Son. With me he is well pleased. No ifs about it. Nothing can remove me from right relatedness with my Father. I am his Son. I know who I am. And I know whose I am. And his Spirit led me here; this is no accidental detour. He led me here, and the One who led me here is going to lead me out. And in the meantime, let's get down to the epic match we came here for."

This life-and-death battle affirmed to the marrow who he was.

No dagger the enemy pulled out of his bag of knives could silence the words of blessing spoken by God, the Father. The desert affirmed Jesus's identity in ways that a walk by a calm, cool stream never could have.

When powerful, religious leaders like Nicodemus seek you out in the dead of night to discover the way to eternal life, you know who you are. When you kneel on holy knees to wash filthy feet, you know who you are. When you steal life from the maw of death, crying out, "Come forth," you know who you are. When you feed five thousand plus, you know who you are. When one of your inner circle betrays you for a bag of silver, you know who you are. And even when you writhe, agonize, and beg for water and become sin itself and cry out with one breath, "My God, my God, why have you forsaken me?" in the next breath you will call out, "Father, into your hands I commit my Spirit."

Father. Father. Father.

You know who you are and whose you are.

Nothing like the desert to show you who and whose you are. And when you know who and whose you are in the desert, when tangible evidence to the contrary is abundant, you know who and whose you are anywhere.

But . . .

But sometimes I don't.

Oh, I can quote the Scripture passages about who I am, and on most days I believe them, but sometimes they seem like mere acquaintances you recognize at the grocery store and wave at across the fruit bins—distantly known, not fellowshiped with in depth. There have been seasons when I have been tempted—mostly in the inky watches of the soul's night—to doubt the goodness of God. I have run smack dab into the power of the conjunction *but*, used to introduce something different or contrasting to what has already been stated.

I know God is good, but . . .

I know he won't abandon me, but . . .

I know no one who trusts in him will be put to shame, but . . .

But.

51

But, I lament. The dark watermark rises. Bad news remains unbalanced by good. I run slowly after fast-fleeing joy. The hoped-for antidote doesn't come. The sting of the sand is my constant companion. Psalm 107 renders the ache this way: "Some wandered in desert wastelands, finding no way to a city where they could settle. They were hungry and thirsty, and their lives ebbed away" (vv. 4–5).

Jesus loves me, this I know, but what about . . .

There, in my desert tent, Jesus speaks to my heart. To shore up the leaky holes of my identity in him—again. At a core, emotional level. Again. Because when the small conjunction of *but* inserts itself into my life experience, I can find it easier to grab ahold of a lie than to cling to the truth that I am the beloved of the Father.

In my own life, the lie often manifests in the common habit of interpreting my life's circumstances. I've always been a sucker for this. Though I know my interpretation of my circumstances is imprecise and faulty, I often equate the favor of God (and dare I say it, even the love of God) with the circumstances in my life. Favorable circumstances mean I am operating in the favor of God. God must really love me. And the dark opposite is also true. If things are difficult or disappointing, God must be turning his face from me. In some way, somewhere, I must not be making the grade.

To be completely frank, I went through a serious chapter in which *but* seemed to be carved into the pages of my life, largely because I misinterpreted circumstances again. And though I know better after three decades of walking with Jesus, I so easily revert to a younger heart; some of the earliest influences in my spiritual life equated performing well with gaining favor of God. To reach my slow-to-learn heart, God often leads me into a place where nothing goes as planned—or even as hoped—so that he can reteach such astonishing truth: his love is not for sale. I can't buy it with my good acts or my right behavior. And that no circumstances—good or ill—can stand in as the symbol of his love for me.

There in the desert, when I have nothing to give and everything is hollowed out, I understand his immutable, unassailable love for me. And the conjunction of *but* loses its right to turn the rudder of my spiritual life.

Knowing that you are hidden in God in Christ (Colossians 3:3) and that the immutable love of God remains (Romans 8) will prepare you for whatever difficult twists and turns remain around life's corner. Even if the enemy himself were to show up by your bedside, whisper his deviant half-truth *ifs* and *buts* into your ear, you, like Jesus, will understand at a core level your deep belovedness.

This is my Son, whom I love; with him I am well pleased.

The wizened and wild desert will have given you this unusual gift. Nothing compares to knowing who you are—and whose you are—to prepare you for whatever is coming next. The desert comes before destiny.

No ifs and buts about it.

When the work of the desert was done, destiny awaited Jesus. He walked into a synagogue, opened a scroll, and declared himself to be the coming One.

The coming One who had come by way of the desert. Who had been prepared by its sandy ministry, to the very marrow.

Reflections

In the beginning there are a great many battles and a good deal of suffering for those who are advancing toward God and afterward ineffable joy.

Syncletica, desert mother [5]

Looking back on your desert seasons or on the particular desert chapters in your life, have you seen God's fingerprints on them? Have you ever encountered the ifs *and* buts, particularly difficult when in a dry, spiritual season? How did God assure you of his love for you and shore up your identity in him during such a time? How did this prepare you for future assignments with Christ? Can you take a tentative step toward believing that on the other side of the desert is destiny?

4

Provision

"We do not regard bread and salt as indispensable." So they were strong for the work of God.

John, desert father[1]

Meanwhile his disciples urged him, "Rabbi, eat something." But he said to them, "I have food to eat that you know nothing about." Then his disciples said to each other, "Could someone have brought him food?"

John 4:31–33

When I was a freshly minted believer in Jesus, circa 1989, I was all about "God doing a new thing." That phrase was in the contemporary Christian ether of the time, and I grabbed it like a teenager grabs the last crust of pizza. I sang it. I wrote it with the attendant exclamation points. If cool Christian T-shirts had been a big thing back then, I would have worn that phrase in every color the late eighties/ early nineties would have produced. But since our Christian T-shirt choices back then were fairly limited, I did what I could in other obsessive ways. I knew God was doing a new thing. Everywhere. In every way! If I prayed or talked deeply with others during those years, you can be certain I worked my "new thing" philosophy in somewhere, somehow. And my life verse, Isaiah 43:19, which says, "Behold, I am doing a new thing; now it springs forth, do you not perceive it?" (ESV), gave me biblical backing for my new obsession.

As embarrassing as this is to admit, I never looked at the full context of that Scripture passage until six years ago, when I started to unpack my own desert experience. Although our God is more than capable of doing a new thing, any ol' time, any ol' way, the new thing he is talking about in Isaiah is contained in the line *following* his beautiful promise to do something new. Sometimes a girl just needs to keep reading.

> Behold, I am doing a new thing;
>> now it springs forth, do you not perceive it?
> I will make a way in the wilderness
>> and rivers in the desert. (Isa. 43:19 ESV)

The new thing that God is doing—among other astounding things—is making a way in the wilderness and rivers in the desert. He is providing in a place where one would least expect it. Rivers don't usually rush through the middle of a desert land. Wilderness lands don't usually have passable highways running through them. Not unless God is the One providing the water and the way. The provision God offers is above the natural. It's supernatural. But that is exactly the new thing God promises he is doing. Our resource is from the Source himself.

God always provides. Even in the desert. Perhaps especially in the desert. If you are there right now, I want you to scrawl that across your own solitary experience. You will be provided for. And God's provision will often be beyond your ability to grasp, beyond your ability to create, and more sustaining than you can dare dream.

Provisional Quality

At events, I sometimes ask if the women there have ever been so lucky as to have their munchkins scramble up a breakfast for them on Mother's Day or attempt to make breakfast for the whole family. Many people reply in the affirmative. From my very scientific surveys, I understand that this breaking of the fast can be culinary fabulousness or more like a full-blown culinary disaster. For some, the tray comes loaded down with gastric gifts such as underdone eggs paired with slices of over-done toast, each arrayed with three huge chunks of still-hard butter and thin trails of jelly. And the coffee. Let us refrain from speaking of it.

But I guarantee you this: any mom or dad worth their runny eggs will gulp those meals down with all the graciousness in the world. The quality, or lack thereof, of the food makes no difference because it's not about the food but about the food maker. The whole thing comes down to the thought behind the gift.

But go with me for a second here. What if this culinary parade went on for not just one meal but day after day, week after week, month after month, until mama—and the whole family—had a serious case of scurvy and anemia to boot? No antioxidant-rich berries. No cruciferous veggies. At some point, no matter how cute you think your kids' offerings might be, things would have to change. "I'm partial to your cheffy self and your preciousness and all, but it's time for this mama to put the apron back on."

You'd throw down the mama card.

Sometimes, in the same way, and for the same reasons, I believe God throws down the Good Father card, in effect saying, "It's time to hand over the spatula, kid. After a long season of allowing you to continue on your own provision, I'm stepping in. You are feeding yourself junk food, but you don't know that, and you're shriveling away inside. You're eating empty calories, spiritually speaking, and the only way I'm going to show you that is if I take over the duties." When that happens, I scrape my watery grits into the disposal, because the Master Chef has come.

Though I don't say it out loud very often, I think of myself as a semi-expert in self-provision. If I have a need, I can usually fill it. That's one of the gifts (and hidden curses) of being a middle-class human being in the Western world. Let's take being thirsty. No sweat. We've got everything from humdrum water fountains to probiotic kombucha to pressed grass juice to diet soda. Not every choice has the same nutritional quality, does it? And in my thinking brain, I know that. Yet all too often, because I run at a dizzying pace, I grab the diet soda. Left to myself, because of my personal bent toward "fast," I choose a thing that, though quick, won't sustain me in the long haul. I slake the thirst and often don't touch the dehydration.

The same thing can happen spiritually if we're not careful. What's quick? What's available? What tickles the felt emotional/spiritual need? We scratch the itch with what's available, fill the ache the best we can, but very often we Band-Aid a gaping wound. We throw vitamins at something that needs serious medicine. We do the best we can at provision, but it's not the best that *Jehovah Jireh* (God, our Provider) can do.

All too often, we won't know this unless something—or Someone—steps in and interrupts our pattern of subtle and stubborn self-provision. So God takes the lead and says, "It's time to visit the desert, where an unexpected gift is at work."

Holy Lack

When was the last time you heard a sermon on lack? Same here. Mostly, we want the overflowing cup, the greater things, the embarrassing riches. And while there is certainly no way to contain (or stop) God's evident goodness toward us, biblically I see that holy lack can also be the pathway to outsized provision. When we are touched with lack in a natural sense, we can discover that in Christ we lack no good thing. Previously, we took a quick gander at Deuteronomy in chapter 2, but let's come in for a fuller examination.

> Remember how the LORD your God led you all the way in the wilderness these forty years, to humble and test you in order to know what was in your heart, whether or not you would keep his commands. He humbled you, *causing you to hunger* and then feeding you with manna, which neither you nor your ancestors had known, to teach you that man does not live on bread alone but on every word that comes from the mouth of the LORD. (Deut. 8:2–3)

59

A phrase in this passage sort of stuns me. Don't miss it. "Causing you to hunger."

The passage says that God caused his children to hunger so that he could feed them. He touched the children of Israel with the unusual gift of natural hunger so that they could learn something that would not have come to them in any other way. God made them empty so that he could fill them. He touched them with lack so that he could fill up what was lacking.

In the desert terrain, this lack can feel terrifying. When I entered a desiccated land, I wanted my creature comforts. I wanted to fill my spiritual belly with the junk food that hit me with happy and released the feel good. "God, if you've led me to such a hard place, the least you can do is let me eat my fill with what I want, right?" We want what we want, and we want it pronto. But God is a better Father than that.

He knows that spiritual health isn't just about avoiding *lesser* bread but also about partaking of *greater* Bread—which is the very word that proceeds from God's mouth. Holy lack always has a purpose, and it is to teach his chosen people that there is a greater Source that will not fail, a Source whose *very word* can provide manna and quail . . . and so much more.

In the desert, often God is saying, "Hand over that jerky stick so I can provide filet mignon."

Listen to the prophet Nehemiah speak of God's provision in the desert hundreds of years after the children of Israel had sojourned for forty long years.

> Because of your great compassion you did not abandon them in the desert. By day the pillar of cloud did not cease to guide

them on their path, nor the pillar of fire by night to shine on the way they were to take. You gave your good Spirit to instruct them. You did not withhold your manna from their mouths, and you gave them water for their thirst. For forty years you sustained them in the desert; they lacked nothing, their clothes did not wear out nor did their feet become swollen. (9:19–21)

Touched with human lack, they lacked nothing in God. Desert walker, the same is offered to you. No matter how fearsome the conditions of your desert, God's provision will not run dry. And his provision will be of the highest quality. Check out the quality goods God offers in your desert excursion:

Compassion. Guidance. Illumination. Instruction. Water. Clothing.

And a little something called manna.

Desert Manna

When I heard about manna while growing up in my church, I mostly wondered about its taste and consistency. Maybe, like me, you thought the whole thing sounded like frosted flakes? I always imagined the Israelites filling up bowls with cereal, sans milk. From Scripture, we definitively know that manna was somewhat sweet—"like coriander seed, white, and the taste of it was like wafers made with honey" (Exod. 16:31 ESV). Sounds like the kind of morsels I'm scrounging for about forty-five minutes after dinner, when my sweet tooth starts talking to me.

But manna was so much more than a sweet tooth hit. Since God's Word talks about manna in many ways, even calling Jesus the bread that comes down from heaven, let's take a closer look at the unique provision God gave to his chosen people as they weathered the desert.

All in a Day's Work

In the desert the whole community grumbled against Moses and Aaron. The Israelites said to them, "If only we had died by the LORD's hand in Egypt! There we sat around pots of meat and ate all the food we wanted, but you have brought us out into this desert to starve this entire assembly to death."

Then the LORD said to Moses, "I will rain down bread from heaven for you. The people are to go out each day and gather enough for that day. In this way I will test them and see whether they will follow my instructions. On the sixth day they are to prepare what they bring in, and that is to be twice as much as they gather on the other days." (Exod. 16:2–5)

The people of God began their exodus with a round of murmuring and complaining against God's provisional ability, wondering if he really had the goods "to prepare a feast in the desert" (Ps. 78:19 ISV). God didn't like the insinuation—spoken, ironically, in the Valley of Sin—that the One who had delivered them from four hundred years of slavery would take them into the desert to starve. The accusation that he would not care for them in such a basic way was met with the stern hand of God. He didn't cotton to the fact that his past faithfulness meant so little to his people or that they longed so dearly for their well-fed enslavement, so God said that to "test them," he would touch them with lack and provide them manna, which had to be gathered in a very specific way.

Except on the seventh day, manna had to be scooped up daily. And one was to take only what was needed for oneself and the people in one's tent. This manna would be preserved, meeting the people's nutritional needs with no spoilage. But if a gatherer took more than was needed for a regular day, the manna would transform into a teeny compost pile before their eyes: wormy and stinky. Simply put, the manna would rot. What was held over would not hold over. The people had to trust God to deliver it daily. And trusting daily for such a basic need was a trust test of the highest order.

Sometimes I find it easy to quietly disparage God's people for such a lack of trust. *People, don't you remember the frogs, the blood, the Angel of Death?* And then I imagine God doing something similar in my own world. What if God asked me to swing open my fridge door one fine morning, only to discover a perfectly God-designed meal for the day? I'd consume it, of course, and get about life with a thankful and full belly. The next day, knowing that I had not taken a trip to the local grocery store, what if God asked me to approach the fridge, *trusting* that he had perfectly filled it with a perfect meal again? That's daily trust. And daily trust can be a doozy.

God's children had to lean into the goodness of God enough not to hoard his provisions from one day to the next. They had to trust that their thirst would be satisfied. They had to believe that they would not wake up to a day that God couldn't handle. Or provide completely for. All of this daily trust was reflected in Jesus's prototypical prayer: "Give us today our daily bread" (Matt. 6:11). There is something distinctly powerful about asking for and gathering manna daily.

Crammers and Hoarders

I have a hoarder's heart. When I have not been diligent in daily bread gathering and finally wake from my half-alive state after subsisting on a starvation diet, I begin to cram and hoard, trying to fill the spiritual stomach too long empty. It is then that I look for the conference or the podcast or the book—or maybe all three in one fine day—and I gorge, forgetting that if I would gather daily, according to God's heart and plan, I would never have too little. Or too much. In God's economy, the daily gatherer has enough. Perfectly enough. No gorging, hoarding, or cramming necessary.

I remember a voice teacher in college who said something I will never forget. She said she could always tell whether a voice student crammed for an hour right before the lesson or practiced for fifteen minutes daily. She said there was no comparison in the result. The daily practitioner was more at ease and had moved from mere memorization to true musicality. The music was in them. It was integrated and unforced. The benefits of daily practice were incredibly numerous, and my coach could always tell who practiced daily and who crammed. I took her piece of advice to heart and internally vowed to follow it. I did so for a while and then relapsed like any college kid running on fumes—cramming, hoarding.

Even on the edge of perimenopause, I sometimes find my collegiate self reemerging. I have to remind myself of the power of gathering God's manna daily. Day-old bread will never do.

I know this. I've thought this. I've been taught this. Yet because we are not so different from our Jewish forebearers, I find myself eschewing the simple commands: Gather daily. Feast daily. Trust daily.

What sustained us yesterday cannot sustain us today. The God who provides manna has made sure of it. As Jesus says, each day has its own troubles. It also has triumphs. Tragedies. Tribulations. And it is the bread we gather daily that will meet the need and the hunger of each new day.

What Is This?

One of the things that has always amused me is the meaning of the word *manna*. It means simply "What is this?" or "What is it?" Now, obviously, this is a tip of the hat to the fact that the children of Israel had never "seen such of a thing," to quote my grandmother Cleola. Can't you imagine them going out the first morning after the dew dried, with whatever baskets they needed to gather enough to fill up the tummies in their tents, picking up the flaky stuff, looking at one another in disbelief, and whispering, "What is this stuff?"

Many Christians today equate manna with the reading of Scripture, and while that is certainly manna the likes of which we cannot survive without, I wonder if doing so puts too limited a definition to the word *manna*. Technically, manna is whatever sustenance God provides daily. Now, obviously, the Bible spiritually fulfills this definition. We can (and should) open God's narrative daily and allow it to feed our very souls. Prayer is communicative, relational manna. Daily exchange with our Maker prepares us to face the hurdles and hurrahs of every day. These are daily mannas, and their importance cannot be overstated.

When I was in my own desert season, I had to ask God, aside from prayer and Scripture, "What is it? What is my manna, God? What are you providing as I sit here on the couch barely able to move, the fear of losing a miracle always on my mind, along with a few hundred other things I haven't looked at in a long while. What's going to get me through this, Jesus? What is my manna—my food—in this particular desert? What comes daily from your hand? What is it? This supernatural experience (weathering the desert) requires your supernatural provision. Give me the bread of heaven—that I have never known, that I will gather daily, and that I trust will come again in the morning hours. This is the provision I know I have never tasted. I will be looking for it each and every morning."

My Own Manna

Click and clack. Yep, click and clack.

That became the answer to my own "What is it?" question. Clicking and clacking on computer keys became my daily manna on that leather sofa. Writing and writing some more. At first, the white space of the computer screen seemed to mirror the desert in my soul. Vast. Expansive. Intimidating. Waiting to be filled. But as I began to write—as the black figures appeared letter by letter, word by word—I realized that *this was a portion of my manna*, on the screen and, ultimately, in my soul. During the hours of intense quiet and solitude, I took out my computer and wrote my heart out, and wrote out my heart. As I did, I experienced God's fonted manna for me.

Specifically, I was working on my first novel, a novelization of a musical I had written. The journey was both difficult and invigorating. I had certain ideas of how the book would take shape, thinking I could render it as it had done on stage. But music and visuals are hard to lasso to earth and wrangle into

words, so to capture the space and the symbol of the musical, I found myself writing my way into a far-off land, a land
of intertestamental wonders, spiritual twists and turns, and a
decades-long love story, all rounded out by the ever-present
voice of Jesus. The book was called *The Magdalene(s)*.

Even though the novel wouldn't make a debut in any tradi-
tional way, it accomplished something even more important,
even more sustaining in my desert and in my life: it schooled
me in something I didn't know I would need. I see now that
the daily manna of writing was teaching me to write in a new
and novel way. I was being trained, without even knowing it,
for all the writing that would come after—for my first nonfic-
tion offering, for this very book, for all the teachings I would
compose as God opened doors of ministry opportunity. God
was priming the desert pump. God was giving me daily manna
to carry me and equip me.

His desert provision was actually sustenance for the vision
that was yet to come. In effect, God was saying, "Here, kid.
Click clack those QWERTY keys. Write every day. Write in me
every day, and doing so will help you weather the difficulty of
this scorching desert season. And though you won't recognize
it now, my daily manna is accomplishing something in you and
for you that you won't see until much later. My provision is in
reality pro-vision, for the vision is yet to be."

God's desert provision was *pro*-vision. My manna was, in
many ways, actually benefiting the coming vision; it was preparing me for the promise that was yet to come. The manna
in the wilderness did the same for the Israelites. It sustained a
people group for the Promised Land. It trained them in trust.
Every day that they rose to gather God's miraculous food they
were flexing their internal trust muscles.

Holy Rations

When you go into the desert, when you are touched with the gift of spiritual lack for a season, you receive an unexpected desert blessing, friend. It's a gift that no one can ever take away from you, and it's a gift I'm not sure you can get any other way. Lack is the open door to God's provision. Daily trust sets the table for you to ingest the holy rations of God. Because God is relentless in getting to the great work of the heart in the desert, he will sustain you during that great work with holy manna, the holy "What is it?" of God.

The desert is where unbelief surrenders and God's provision reigns supreme. In the desert, God is the Source of resource. He is the well that never runs dry.

Reflections

The same *abba* (desert father) said, "We went to another old man who detained us for a meal and he offered us oil of horse radish." We said to him, "Father, give us a little good oil." At these words he crossed himself and said, "I didn't know there was any other kind."[2]

I've spent a good deal of time looking through one of the definitive compilations of the sayings of the desert fathers and mothers, compiled by Benedicta Ward in 1975. At first, I was surprised (though I shouldn't have been) by how many of the quotes and stories revolved around food. In hindsight, I should have expected this. Since these people had left everything and moved into the desert, most of them in complete poverty, it follows that food and water would have been a consuming concern. Some of the stories regarding the desert meals are fantastical. Some are practical. Some are deeply ascetic. Some, like the mini-story above, are quite workaday. To my mind, this quotation expresses the human reality that the heart wants what the heart wants. It appears that the unnamed abba was requesting some good (or better) oil—something different than this "oil of horse radish" (which does not sound appealing on any level). And then Benjamin, a desert father, replies with the quippy, "I didn't know there was any other kind of oil in the desert." In other words, what we have is enough. If horseradish oil is what we have, then it is exactly what we need from God's hand. It is good oil.

What "good oil" has God provided for you in your desert experience? What manna? Was it an expected provision, or was it a surprising one? Have you ever experienced holy lack that only God could fill? How is the quality of your daily, spiritual provision?

5

Perspective

Another of the old men questioned Amma Theodora saying, "At the resurrection of the dead, how shall we rise?" She said, "As pledge, example, and as prototype we have him who died for us and is risen, Christ the Lord."

Theodora, in *The Sayings of the Desert Fathers*[1]

Teach us to number our days,
    that we may gain a heart of wisdom.

Psalm 90:12

*I*f you were to poke around my house—say, back in the back of the office, on a bookshelf where the evidence of my family lies—you might find the object. It's a beautiful glass square, probably created to be a fancy planter—one of those in which the tangled roots are as much a part of the arrangement as the plants above the soil line. I don't quite remember how it came to me, but there it is now, filled to the brim . . . with sand. South Carolina sand to be exact, taken from a visit to Pelion, a small town in the sandhills of South Carolina, a visit I wrote about ten years ago:

You can get a sunburn in half a minute in the sandhills of Pelion, South Carolina. The sun's rays seem to invert and come up at you from the greedy center of the earth, beaming straight through the super-heated sand beneath your unmanicured feet. It's a Carolina desert. It's a blazing hot sandy shore, without any ocean in sight.

That's how it feels in Florence Baptist Church's pre–Civil War cemetery. Nary a shade-giving tree. The sun shines perennially, always haughty. Headstones dot the landscape, marble testaments to lives that ended their long (or short) journey there. There are so many babies—a reminder of a time when giving birth, as it still is in so many parts of the world, was a life-threatening event. And young soldiers from too many wars—starting with the Civil War. Unless you've steeled yourself beforehand, it can shatter your heart to walk around the generational-tapestry of rest.

Soon, I will be standing at Patsy Crout's marker, a brass plate sunken in the sand.

I forgot to put the days of her birth and death on the gravestone. How in the world does the oldest daughter, the only daughter, forget that? She was born on October 31, 1940. Halloween isn't a date difficult to remember. And she died on June 16, around the time the nurse said she would, when my brother and I were numb with the shock of it all. But all her marker says is

72

October 1940–June 2005. It is as if the days—the bright day of her birth and the dim day of her death—were too painful to memorialize.

Mom had told Jim and me that it would likely be "a year and a half." We sobbed and grieved and searched the internet, calling each other at odd intervals throughout the day, whispering, "That seems awfully long for pancreatic cancer. Maybe the cancer is stage 1 or something?" I waited about a week to come because she wanted me there for the start of chemo.

I got a speeding ticket on the way down, and the squat patrolman left me sobbing by the side of I-65, probably thinking what a good actress I was playing the cancer, mom-dying, desperate-to-get-there card. He drove off without so much as glancing back or letting me off with just a warning, leaving me slumped over the wheel, being vacuumed in and out each time an 18-wheeler rolled by my little minivan.

I remember making it home and rushing up the stairs, and there she was, already in the bed, early in the evening. I sat down on the bed's edge and cried. I remember her singsonging, "Well, honey, honey"—a bit of surprise mixed with the sharp bite of beholding your child's wild grief. She sat there, the dying one, comforting me. Her frame was branch thin. Winter had come where there should have been fall. Every wiry hair was blanched of all color, and her brown eyes were growing dull. Petite chocolate marbles.

I couldn't embrace her at that moment because I couldn't embrace the moment. To embrace the moment meant to embrace her death.

Neither of us was ready to speak aloud the conversation our hearts were already having. And so I stroked her hand, memorizing it. She was already flirting with the angels, and

I was heavy-laden, tied to the earth. She was a kite on the high windy chop, and I was a kid desperately trying to reel her back in.

These things I remember.

During that trip to Florence Baptist Church, I collected a baggie of sand—from the place where she lay—and brought it home to the aforementioned funky glass container, where it remains as a reminder of the terrible, exquisite gifts the desert of loss gave, the greatest of which was the gift of perspective. Oh, how God revealed my heart by forcing me to look hard at its skewed perspective.

Death's desert taught me the absolute necessity of considering the end.

In the Beginning, the End

It was the best of times. It was the worst of times.

It is a truth universally acknowledged that a single man in possession of a fortune, must be in want of a wife.

Call me Ishmael.

Without reading ahead, many of you can probably identify the novels from which these first lines are taken.

A Tale of Two Cities. Pride and Prejudice. Moby Dick.

I often wonder what level of artistic alchemy was at work in Dickens, Austen, and Melville that allowed them to deliver such otherworldly firstfruits to us. Somehow they captured something of the entirety of their master works in a few words—in one or two sentences. Somehow the entirety of the stories is contained in them. Somehow every twist and turn was penned down by the pen. What majestic beginnings.

We instantly recognize a great beginning, don't we? We pay special attention to the beginning of a song or a talk or even the way a competitive swimmer gets off the block.

But do our endings receive as much care? As much notice? Dare I say, as much love? Not so much.

Check this out:

It is a far, far better thing that I do, than I have ever done; it is a far, far better rest that I go to, than I have ever known.

Darcy, as well as Elizabeth, really loved them, and they were both ever sensible of the warmest gratitude towards the persons who, by bringing her into Derbyshire, had been the means of uniting them.

It was the devious-cruising Rachel, that in her retracing search after her missing children, only found another orphan.

Those are the last lines of the same world-famous classic pieces of literature. Surely they were as labored over and loved on as the first ones. Surely the authors—who began so well, so carefully—finished as circumspectly. I bet a hundred sixpence that Jane Austen labored as much over the final words of *Pride and Prejudice* as she did its indelible beginning.

But somehow endings don't scribble themselves on our souls as deeply. Except on very rare occasions, we don't rush to Etsy-fy

T-shirts with them. In my very unscientific interweb study, you'll find a boatload more search requests for the first line of a great literary work than for the last line. Poor, unconsidered endings.

And in the real world, we do something similar, don't we? We often neglect our endings. We hurry them along, minimize them, sometimes even reject them outright. And when they happen—and they happen to us all—usually we scurry to get to the next beginning.

Just as every beginning embodies potential and promise and birth itself, so every little ending—*in some way*—embodies the ultimate ending of an earthly life. So starting over is a much safer (and cheerier) endeavor, perhaps forestalling the knowledge that we all face difficult endings. Of the job. Of the friendship. Of the ministry appointment. Of earthly life itself.

If you search "the end" and "Ted Talks," you will quickly see that talks about the end of life, or what happens in the end, or how to prepare for the end are among the most watched videos.[2] Culturally, we have caught up to something the Bible states boldly in Ecclesiastes: "It is better to go to a house of mourning than to go to a house of feasting, for death is the destiny of everyone; the living should take this to heart" (7:2). As a young woman, when I first heard a preacher at my home church talk about the importance of paying attention to the end—at a funeral—I admit, I recoiled a bit. Through tears, as he read those hard words about a house of mourning, I wanted to be anywhere but. As he talked about taking the end to heart, I shifted uncomfortably in my chair. I was too young to grasp the wisdom of these verses. But, years later, as I faced my mother's death, I began to understand the richness of those Scriptures and what he had planted deep into the soil of my heart. And in an odd way, as I grew in Christ, these hard words grew on me.

When my mother was diagnosed with pancreatic cancer and I ventured into the wild and agonizing desert of her three-month sojourn home, I learned for the first time what it was to sit down with a finale.

It was the first time I had considered the end and what perspective-shifting gifts the end could give my heart as a daughter losing her mother and as a young mother just beginning the mothering.

Watch the Way You Watch

Perspective is defined like so: a particular attitude toward or way of regarding something; a point of view.[3]

I'm particularly partial to the second half of the definition, because in acting school, one of the techniques we were trained in was making certain the character we played had a specific point of view on the events and story in which they were involved. I remember numerous times teachers asking me, "What's this character's point of view?" Or even, "Allison, have you given your character a POV for this scene?" Possessing a strong point of view meant the character had a particular opinion on the circumstances and happenings. A particular slant. Not having a point of view at all was considered extremely lazy in my school. Point of view was often a most basic starting place for character development.

We all have specific points of view, even if we are unaware of them. Often, POVs are formed from years and years of experience on earth. Your experiences, your family, your temperament, your social groups—all these things influence your point

77

of view/perspective. Think of it this way. If a person views the world thinking that at any moment the ax will fall, most of their experiences will be marked with caution and perhaps a hint of negativity. Conversely, if a person views the world thinking that every day is an unexpected kiss, well then, most of their experiences will be marked with the spark of hopefulness and expectation. Point of view, or perspective, is a powerful force.

One of my favorite prayers from Paul includes his intercession for the way we see: "I pray that the eyes of your heart may be enlightened in order that you may know the hope to which he has called you, the riches of his glorious inheritance in his holy people" (Eph. 1:18). Beautifully, Paul is praying for the Ephesians' hearts. And in a very real way, he is praying for their hearts' points of view. He doesn't want the eyes of their hearts to miss the incredible blessings right in front of them or to stare at lesser things, like squabbling over what color to paint the Ephesian fellowship hall. He says, "Raise your eyes! Look up higher!" He wants them to possess a perspective of hope; he wants them to view their great inheritance in one another. He's praying for the way they see.

That's a prayer I need someone to pray for me every day of the week and then some.

Altering the way we see is no easy task. It's one thing to don a perspective for character work on the stage. It's another thing altogether to shift a deeply held perspective in real life. Personally, I believe our peculiar points of view are as ingrained as our heights. Often, a shift in perspective happens at obvious life-altering events, such as birth, marriage, divorce, death. Even national events can cause a shift in perspective. 9/11 was one such event in recent history that caused a particular shift societally, politically, and militarily. Shift is difficult and usually comes out of—or after—the most difficult and tumultuous events.

The desert can give us the same shift in perspective, if we dare to surrender to it. I spoke of the first peg of our desert tent as being the revelation of our hearts. To be sure, a stubborn heart like mine needed something like the "desperate" of the desert, where extreme, often unrelenting circumstances forced me to take a hard gaze at the particular perspective through which I looked at life. I needed to cry uncle. I needed the courage, the willingness to switch those spectacles out for some different ones.

The desert experience of my mother's all-too-quick homegoing forced me to consider doing just that.

Caught and Taught

My mother had been taught by the best how to rightly consider the end.

Once, I remember on a visit to Pelion joining in a family ritual: the washing of the dishes. My grandma and grandpa never had a dishwasher, and so, after her incredible Southern dinners, we all took turns scraping, washing, drying, and restocking all the dinnery things. On this particular wash line night, my grandma uncharacteristically disappeared from the kitchen and went to a back room where she stored frozen veggies and meats and all manner of boxes of unknown things. It was grandma's emporium. When she returned, she said, as if she were giving a report on the state of her garden, "When I die, I want you to sing this at my funeral, Allison." She then proceeded to hand me a ripped-out page of a hymnal. At the top, emboldened in ink, it said—brace yourself—"At the End of the Road." She looked at me and continued, "I want you to sing this song and 'Amazing Grace.'" I have a vague recollection of some family members protesting, "Ma-ah! Come on, Ma-ah." I do remember the shocked look of my own mother. Cleola didn't bat a Southern eyelash. She just went back to cleaning up the remains of a ham hock and lima bean dinner. That was that. An important piece of business had been discussed, witnessed, and finalized.

To be clear, she was the least morbid person I ever knew. People adored her. Wanted to be near her. Admired her. When I was younger, my favorite jaunt on earth was a walk to my grandparents' mailbox. It was planted in the sand at the end of a long trail through a little stand of trees that grew into a perfect, sun-shaded arch. We would walk to the mailbox, and she would talk. On several occasions, I recall that she mentioned wanting Jesus to take her in her sleep, and she wanted me to know—needed me to know—that she was absolutely unafraid of death. Meeting Jesus had given her peace. Unassailable peace in life. Unassailable peace in death, whenever it would come. I shouldn't have been surprised at the ease with which she spoke of the end of her earthly life that day in the kitchen.

I have since learned that as a young woman, my grandmother— whom I loved to watch pluck wild blackberries from the bushes at the end of her road—had washed the bodies of the community's departed that were laid out in my great-great aunt's house. This may sound graphic, but it was actually a great grace. There were no embalmers in that day and age, and so the final preparation of the body fell to the family or to the people of the community, who considered it a duty and an honor and a final act of love. They swaddled babies at birth, and they swaddled bodies at death. Apparently, Cleola had been considering the end from a very young age. She also had the blessing of attending a pre–Civil War church, Florence Baptist Church, which had a graveyard right next door to it. Four generations of my people are buried there, including my mother.

It strikes me that my mother's mother lived in a world marked by churches, bridges, and graveyards—not a bad way to mark a life. And we live in a world marked by malls, highways, and GPS coordinates. No wonder we sometimes get a little lost on the way, and no wonder that people in my grandmother's day more often seemed to know where they were going and what the journey to the end could look like.

She had given the special perspective of considering the end to my mom, who, in turn, gave it to me.

Back to Mom

In her desert experience, with the end approaching, Mom began talking. And the things she said pushed hard against the perspective I was living with.

We had conversations that I do not believe we would have had if she had not been facing eternity. Her fears, her hopes, and, poignantly, the deep questions she carried around about the quality of her mothering. She spoke of these topics as openly, as innocently, as she might have once asked me to pick up her favorite chicken salad and sweet tea.

She was dying. We could no longer deny it. And the dying made her brave—brave enough to say the things and ask the questions that a long life might have never required of her. And being faced with these questions—questions that only the end dredged up—forced me to lock eyes with this truth: endings not only are guaranteed but also can be for our good—if we allow them to change the way we live our now. This was a crash course in perspective shift. Death, even death in which eternity is secured and sure, sifted everything, and only real treasure remained. Though I wouldn't wish the experience on anyone I love, I would certainly wish its rich gift of shifted perspective.

Enlightening and telling to me were that her most urgent thoughts and questions were about how she had used her life for Jesus and how she had mothered my brother and me. In the end, two important things: Jesus and family. Here we were, my brother and I, thirty-one and thirty-five, respectively, and she was still chewing on whether she had done enough to mother us well. If she had given us enough wind to be able to raise the sails without her. If there were particular deficits and/or strengths she had left us with. I know every mother frets over her children, no matter their age, but there was more ballast to it than that, somehow. She was concerned about the *substance* of her mothering, as if she were taking a beautifully aged tapestry and flipping it over so that all the thread and knots could be examined for what they were. I have never been asked more bald-faced, perspective-shifting questions. Honestly, I never saw it coming. At thirty-five, I had long since ceased thinking of myself as someone still in need of mothering in any substantive way.

The desert of loss was gifting to me a new heart perspective. *Pay attention to what people talk about at the end. Pay attention.* Pay attention and look at your perspective.

At that point, I had never stopped to consider the quality of my own mothering (I only had an eighteen-month-old after all), and I had certainly never stopped to consider the lasting legacy the quality of my mothering could leave on any future children God would gift us with—future children who would grow into future adults.

To be frank, I have never considered myself a "total" natural at mothering. That is definitely uncomfy to type, but the truth is still true no matter how squirmy it makes a gal. I remember watching women I considered innately gifted with the mother gene and secretly thinking, *How do they do that?* Mothering, for me, is like my relationship with dance: I have to work at it for a while before it integrates into my body. I used to joke with one of my much younger friends, Mindy, about being my mom mentor. I would learn from her easy way with kids and try to glean insights for myself.

I adore my sons to the moon and back. I've got a mama bear inside me the size of a morbidly obese grizzly. I would lasso the moon for my "Tick-Tock" and "Luke the Red" if a mere mortal could do so, and I think regularly about how I could mother them in better ways. But still, mothering remains a holy challenge—one that requires leaning into the grace of Christ. I return to my mom's desert perspective over and over again, as she offered the severe gifts only mortality can deliver, and they revealed my heart to the very DNA. Her perspective-shifting gift remains a holy plumb line for my life: *Remember the closest relationships. Remember the mothering.* In the end, this will be the only question on your lips: How well did I love those closest to me?

Once, during a period when I was particularly worried about the world my older son would grow into, I asked, "Lord, what kind of world will Levi inherit?"

And like a lightning bolt, I heard, "Whatever world you give to him."

I can count on one hand the times I have heard the unmistakable, internal voice of Christ, and this was one of them. In that one sentence, it was as if God were reminding me, "Remember the gift your mother gave you while she waited for me to bring her home." It was as if he were saying: *Remember the end.*

....

Remember the mothering.

Remember that the things at the top of your to-do list will never be more important than the people on your to-love list.

Remember this hard, desert blessing.

When you are in a dehydrated place and all feels boiled down to one dry bone, remember that tomorrow is not promised. You learned this younger than many. You have walked through death's valley, shadowed and sandy, my rod and my staff your guide. The most severe desert gifts dwell there, hidden and austere. Beauty is there too, if you dig for it. Your heart needs this beautification, the beauty of a shifted perspective.

Go into the desert and be changed there. Your heart's eyes changed. Changed like the sands of the desert, shifting the topography of the earth itself. You will not emerge the same. Your eyes will see differently.

....

Back to the Couch

Years later, in another desert—on a leather couch, while Luke the Red gestated within me—I remembered my mother. Patsy. It was six years after she had said the eternal hello to the Lover of her soul, and I still remembered everything.

I remembered that the desert sometimes gives us back our children in the most unexpected ways. Sometimes the desert looks like crying at your mom's feet while she takes her first step onto the eternal streets. Sometimes it looks like sitting as still as stone on a couch so that the life within you has a chance to take the first step at all. Sometimes it means surrendering to the desert, allowing your heart to be revealed, because new life will come forth if you dare to do so.

Oh, the unexpected gift of a desert perspective.

Reflections

Sit in your cell, collecting your thoughts. Remember the day of your death. . . . But keep the day of resurrection and of presentation to God in remembrance also.

Evagrius, desert father[4]

Many of the sayings of the desert fathers and mothers concern their "cells." When I hear the word cell, I think of a jail cell or a weird-looking organism under a microscope. The cells of the desert fathers and mothers were not jail cells, but they were the places they lived in solitude, often caves, huts, or simple stone structures. Writer and thinker Benedicta Ward says it this way: "The cell was of central importance in their asceticism. 'Sit in your cell and it will teach you everything,' they said. The point was that unless a man could find God here, in this one place, his cell, he would not find him anywhere else. But they had no illusions about what it meant to stay in their cell: it meant to stay there in mind as well as body."[5]

In some ways, I think of the desert experience as a cell. If we will "sit in it," it just might change our very heart's perspective.

Have you ever experienced a shift in perspective in the desert? If so, what did it entail? Mine included some deep things about mothering and priority and quality—but yours is likely different. Take a moment to write about the ways "the eyes of your heart" were enlightened during your desert detour.

6

Rest

I have been to sleep, haven't I?

Arsenius, desert father[1]

The LORD replied, "My Presence will go with you, and I
will give you rest."

Exodus 33:14

Jezebel, a woman whose usurping position had been challenged by God and God's prophet, rode the sharp edge of fury. Her false powers and prophets had been reduced to non-existence, and she was in a blood rage, wanting to exact vengeance on one man, the prophet Elijah, who had issued the challenge to her prophets and had won the day, hands down. Jezebel was so committed to her vow of having

Elijah murdered that she made this rash statement regarding her own life: "May the gods punish me and do so severely if I don't make your life like the life of one of them by this time tomorrow!" (1 Kings 19:2 CSB).

You would think that Elijah, the prototypical power prophet, would have sent a scroll back in response with a snarky epistle like so:

> Dearest Queen,
>
> Since the Lord, my God, in whose presence I stand, lit up an altar that had been doused three times with water after your prophets raved and cut themselves to elicit a response from a predictably mum Baal, and since the 450 false prophets have now taken their last breath, you are not in any position to be talkin' threats.
>
> Peripatetically yours,
Elijah

However, the Bible, ever so true to real life and hearts, records Elijah's response to the threat of Jezebel, as well as all that followed after, point by poignant point.

Let's look.

Elijah's Desert Sojourn

Elijah was afraid, so he got up and fled for his life to Beer Sheba in Judah. He left his servant there, while he went a day's journey into the desert. He went and sat down under a shrub and asked the LORD to take his life: "I've had enough! Now, O LORD, take my life. After all, I'm no better than my ancestors." He stretched out and fell asleep under the shrub. All of a sudden an angelic messenger touched him and said, "Get up and eat." He looked and right there by his head was a cake baking on hot coals and a jug of water. He ate and drank and then slept some more. The LORD's angelic messenger came back again, touched him, and said, "Get up and eat, for otherwise you won't be able to make the journey." So he got up and ate and drank. That meal gave him the strength to travel forty days and forty nights until he reached Horeb, the mountain of God. (1 Kings 19:3–8 NET)

Elijah ran a long day's journey into the Negev desert. After Jezebel's demonic threat, Elijah was serious about putting some miles between himself and the furious queen. Something about this particular maniacal menace made Elijah desperate to get outta Dodge (read: the northern kingdom). He sprinted away like an antelope, fleeing deep into the desert.

Eventually, Elijah collapsed under a shrub (or broom tree), begging God to take his life. Don't rush past that, friend. In the canon of God's Scripture, pleading for the One who gave you breath to stop your breath is serious medicine, especially from one so greatly affirmed and utilized as Elijah. Yet he asked God to do the deed, telling him that not much had ever gone right for his familial line, and, if God would see fit, Elijah would like him to end the line with him. "Giver of life," he cried, "take me to my death."

I wonder if Elijah's circumstances seemed so stark that eternity was the only solution he imagined could bring relief? Like Elijah, I've camped there on occasion. Maybe some of you have as well. Likely all of us have heard someone we love proclaim, "I'm just ready to go home now." Even while deeply loving God, we can experience times that cause us to long for the eternal relief of heaven.

Maybe, like Elijah, we've run hard and run out. Joy and hope are like desert mirages—fleeting, wavy in the heat, always a smidge out of reach. We can remember them; we just can't reach them. Threatened one too many times, confused by the outcome of standing for God, we flee into our own version of the Negev and collapse. Another forward step is impossible.

Ever since I dove deep into Elijah's story years ago, I have believed that Elijah was suffering, at least in part, from depression. I'm not alone in this thought. One of my favorite go-to sources for the insights and deductions of scholars, Eerdmans' *The Pulpit Commentary*, describes Elijah's emotional state in vivid blues. Words and phrases such as "profound disappointment," "mortification," "dispirited," and "broken down" snake through the pages of scholarly thought. One writer described Elijah's threatening encounter with the queen as a "death-blow of his hopes."[2]

I have often wondered if this desert flight is perhaps the prototypical narrative of depression in the Bible. We won't know for certain until we enter eternity, but all the ingredients are there. Ingredients like hopelessness ("I've had enough!"), fatigue (exhausted sleep), guilty worthlessness ("My family is nothing and I am nothing"), isolation (he abandons his servant and goes it alone into the desert), longing for final and fatal relief ("End my line with me"). All these ingredients, when thrown into a Crock-Pot, will yield a murky depression stew by the end of the day. Thick enough to stick to your bones. Just give it enough time.

Elijah's broom-tree collapse looks an awful lot like an enemy I've battled in my own life a time or twenty. Except for the sleeping part, I can identify with this "noon-day demon" or acedia, first so-called by the desert fathers and mothers.

His probable depression makes complete and perfect sense to me. Not only am I given to it chemically, not only does it snake up and down the branches of my family tree, but I also understand the unique and painfully tender timing of Elijah's crash. It's the backside backlash. It's the demonic boomerang, sent to sweep the prophet's legs out from under him after quite a victory. Sometimes, I've noticed that the enemy doesn't assault before the adventurous assignment with God. He often viper-strikes after, when we experience the natural letdown. When we're tired. When we question if what we did actually produced lasting kingdom fruit. When the mistakes we made are magnified more than his majesty in our minds.

When the proverbial snake is chomping on our Achilles, getting back up for the next spiritual marathon is quite a challenge.

When we are struggling as deeply as the prophet Elijah did (though our precipitating reasons and events may be quite different from his), we need *to search for* and *submit ourselves to* the unique ways God brings heart restoration in the desert:

heavenly touch
heavenly fuel
heavenly sleep
heavenly rhythms

Heavenly Touch

Maybe like me you remember the terrifying and heart-shredding stories that emerged from the world's orphanages during the

1980s and '90s. The pictures of all those solitary babies in cribs were almost as traumatic as the total, abject lack of sound. No babbles. No coos. No cries. Eerie and enduring quiet. Due to the overwhelming need and the lack of care, precious infants were left untouched, and left untouched for long enough, they ultimately abandoned their cry. Crying became useless because no one was coming to pick them up. And when the cry is lost—the primary mode of communication for a babe—so, somehow, is the desire to live fully. As a result, many of those babes failed to thrive, and this failure was, at least in part, directly related to the lack of human touch and care.[3]

But the coin has a more hopeful side. Think of the optimistic stories of generous folks who volunteer in neonatal intensive care units to rock and hold premature babies, skin to skin. Numerous studies have shown that skin-to-skin contact regulates body temperature, aids with weight gain, and helps to regulate the stress response.[4] In these cases, touch reinforces and encourages life and growth.

Touch has restorative power—which is tenderly reflected in our prophet's poignant narrative.

God sent an angel to minister to Elijah, and the first thing the heavenly messenger did was touch the sleeping man.

Fall into that for a moment. He touched him.

No heraldic announcement. No singing choirs. No ladders with angels ascending and descending. No pillar of fire or cloud of presence. Just a gentle, tender touch on a body that had borne much.

Now, obviously, this gesture might have been about rousing the man from his slumber or letting him come to slowly so he didn't die from a coronary when he discovered that an angel of the living God was hanging out under the broom tree right next to him. But I think, very possibly, something more was occurring. Because the way that angels herald the heralded is often described in great detail (think of Mary's encounter announcing the miraculous pregnancy with Jesus or Isaiah's call to ministry), we have to consider this holy touch as a critical part of the story, mining it for meaning.

The angel touched Elijah in his desert. I've been pondering what that touch could have meant to an obviously distraught and distressed servant of God. First of all, a touch roots us in reality. A touch says we are here right now. A touch lets us know we are not alone. A touch says I am present, right now, with you. A touch gives comfort. A touch says things our words often fail to communicate. A touch often interrupts the cycle of chaos in which we are caught. A touch gives a pained mind something else to focus on, even for a moment. Isn't that why experts have begun to tell us as parents that if we want to truly reach our children, we should touch them on the arm or the shoulder? Isn't that why when a child is inconsolable, often our embrace, not our words, accomplishes calm? Touch is powerful, and no touch is more powerful than the touch of God and his messengers.

Whenever I think of the tender touch of heaven, I immediately see Jesus's outstretched hand. Perhaps you've heard this account from Matthew:

> When Jesus came down from the mountain, large crowds followed Him. And a leper came to Him and bowed down before Him, and said, "Lord, if You are willing, You can make me clean." Jesus stretched out His hand and touched him, saying, "I am willing; be cleansed." And immediately his leprosy was cleansed. (8:1–3 NASB)

The healing was miraculous in and of itself, but so was the touch that preceded it. Jesus's touch was astounding in light of the facts. Leprosy, a fatal and feared disease in ancient times, visited upon its victims such separation, such an apartness from the community, that sufferers had to declare themselves "Unclean! Unclean!" wherever they roamed. A victim was stripped of their identity, often being called in Scripture "a leper." Not "John, who has leprosy" but a leper. John was known by his disease.

So not only was the sufferer sick but the sufferer was also shamed by society and stripped of all identity save the name of the feared disease—adding a ton of bricks to an already unbearable load. Somehow the physical sores, the whitening hair, the loss of appendages seemed almost secondary to a life cloaked in such excoriating, soul-sucking shame.

So here we have the anonymous man, "a leper," getting to Jesus through a crowd. Rather than pressing his way to Christ, as people did in the many other miraculous encounters recorded in the canon, he probably made his way through a curious crowd that parted like the Red Sea as people heard calls of "Unclean! Unclean! Unclean!" I bet they made way all right, watching to see what the Teacher would do for the one so shunned and sick, the one who was the walking dead in their day and time. The leper bowed, a sign of veneration, and made a stunning profession of faith: "Lord, if you are willing, you can make me clean." I wonder if he was speaking a million words contained in that one plea. Words like:

> I know I am only a leper, but even I can recognize you as Lord. You are Lord, even over my condition. I know full well the desperate uncleanness of my state, and I know what the law

says about my nearness to you right now; I know what inconvenience you might have to go through to be near me, and I know it is doubtful that you will be willing to cleanse one like me. But, Lord, oh Lord, you alone can make me clean. If you are willing.

Before answering the leper's agonizing "if" statement, the Messiah stretched out his hand. This was no casual, accidental brush of the fingertips, no whoops-I-didn't-mean-to-excuse-me-pardon-me moment. Jesus made a move to touch the man. He made a deliberate gesture of connection, of human connection. Jesus brought him back into the realm of human community and connectivity in one touch. Did the crowd gasp, holding its collective breath as Jesus deliberately reached out, breaching the distance between himself and the man? Did they step back in revulsion and fear as his hand alighted on the poor, wretched man? I often wonder where Jesus touched him. On his cheek, ravaged by sores and patches? On his head, covered in a wild shock of prematurely white hair? On his bony, burlap-covered shoulder, signifying comfort and comradery?

All we know for certain is that Jesus touched him and the touch changed everything for the man. And it revealed everything about Jesus, the Christ. Not only did it reveal Jesus's lordship over disease and over uncleanness, but it also revealed his lordship over the law and over shame. The touch of Jesus healed the man's lifelong shame before Jesus healed his disease. Jesus healed the outcast's heart before he healed the outcast's health.

I cannot tell you the number of things Jesus touched in my own Desert de Leather Couch, things I will talk about in the next chapter. Things I had been carrying a long time. Things that had bowed me into spiritual exhaustion and spiritual sleep, though to any human eye I seemed quite awake. Things I carried unwittingly into the desert. Things no human hand could ever reach, so hidden were they in the dark soil of my heart and the tangled knot of my mind.

Things that needed the touch of God.

When you are in the desert, don't run from the touch of Jesus. Stay still and wait for the touch that changes everything.

Heavenly Fuel

> And behold, an angel touched him and said to him, "Arise and eat." And he looked, and behold, there was at his head a cake baked on hot stones and a jar of water. And he ate and drank and lay down again. (1 Kings 19:5–6 ESV)

In other words, Elijah, wake up. Wake up, exhausted and ravaged heart. There is one thing needful now. Eat. Drink.

In the desert, baking something was often accomplished by digging a small, circular trough in the sand and lining it with hot stones.[5] We can't say with certainty that the angel of the Lord sat by emptied-out Elijah baking for an hour or two while he slumbered, but the act certainly would have fallen right in line with the incredible care and attention to detail that the angel exhibited toward his near-comatose charge. Whether the angel built an oven and baked the cake or whether it miraculously appeared as the manna once did, the sustenance, the fuel, was there. Available. And near.

Quite near. Do you notice what Scripture records about the position of the cake? The cake was "at his head." At Elijah's head. To my way of imagining the text, Elijah awoke and was so weary that he could only turn his head toward the aromatic, heavenly food.

This reminds me of more occasions than I care to count— back before the flu vaccine—when I seemed to attract every bug known and unknown to man. Countless times my mother would heat up a small mug full of those thin, hard noodles in yellow broth, lift it to my mouth, and instruct me to get something in me so that dehydration wouldn't set in.

"You have to try, Alli. You have to try. Just turn your head. Just sit up enough so it doesn't spill."

Some of us don't know how close the heavenly fuel is for us. We just have to turn our heads.

So often we are out in the dry, desolate places hunting signs and wonders when God is right beside us asking us simply to eat and drink. It is interesting to note the things God used to minister to Elijah in his depleted, and perhaps depressed, state. Water and food. I know from personal experience that when real depression has fallen like a dark cloak over the mind and soul and body, often appetite and self-care go out the window first. The neglect we offer the body reflects the pain in the mind. God, through the angel, knew exactly what to do, and what to do first. Before God addressed the burden of the prophet, he cared for the body of the prophet.

The care exhibited for Elijah's corporeal body is significant for us. All too often we act like modern-day Gnostics, who, along with other odd beliefs, felt the body, like all material things, was evil. And if we don't take the belief as far as all that, we definitely place the body in fourth or fifth place on the spiritual docket. I know I have. I've thought things like, *Well, use it up, blow it out. You can't take it with you.* And while there is a kernel of truth nestled inside that "give it all" thinking, there is also a hidden, spiritualized disdain and devaluation for the form that carries me through life on this earth.

God made our bodies. God cares for our bodies. When God created us, in his image, he tabernacled us in flesh and ran us through with blood. Under the old covenant, many prescriptive and ritual laws concerned the appearance of, the health of, the proper care of, and the value of the body. One of the most important underpinnings of orthodox Christianity is that Jesus came in bodily form—fully God and fully human. First Timothy puts it beautifully: "By common confession, great is the mystery of godliness: He who was revealed in the flesh" (3:16 NASB). Jesus was incarnated not as a little spirit baby with invisible angel wings but as a marriage of flesh and blood like you and me. He was a baby who wet himself and suckled and bawled, and as the years piled on, he became a young man who watched his legs and lip fuzz with hair and perhaps felt his bones stretch and groan as his height came in. On the cross, many of Jesus's cries of agony sprang from the brutality that battered his body. Then Jesus resurrected in bodily form, and this bodily resurrection is a key pillar of our whole faith structure. He told Thomas to touch his physical scars; he cooked and ate fish with his disciples on the shore of Galilee during his forty-day postresurrection ministry. He came in the body; he died in the body; he resurrected in the body.

So it follows that, as Christ followers, you and I are exhorted to care for our bodies and to glorify God with them, as 1 Corinthians encourages: "Do you not know that your bodies are temples of the Holy Spirit, who is in you, whom you have received from God? You are not your own; you were bought at a price. Therefore honor God with your bodies" (6:19–20).

I love the way this passage begins. "Do you not know?" Many of us do not know that this corporeal presence on earth houses the very presence of the Holy Spirit, part of the Triune God. In so many unique ways, our physical bodies matter to God.

So then we should not be surprised that when we, like Elijah, are in a desert, God helps us to tend them with care and physical fuel.

During my own couch desert, I looked forward to one day every week more than any other. It was my once-a-week, get-out-of-jail-free-card medical appointment. All manner of unpredictability and some unpleasant medical procedures often awaited me, but you'd have thought mama was going to the mall for a makeover. Jonathan and I would usually open the car windows, play one of my fave pop ditties too loudly for our ages, grab a drive-thru coffee, and make the minutes and miles stretch there and back. On one of the outings, the medical gurus discovered that, in addition to the aforementioned dumb cervix, I had developed the Big D: gestational diabetes. My AMA (advanced maternal age) had already placed me at greater risk for gestational diabetes, but then added to that were a complete lack of exercise and copious amounts of butter-laced and hand-cooked casseroles.

My physical body needed some care so that the developing body inside me wouldn't grow to the size of a Goliath baby, causing a whole bevy of other complications. Like the inability to give birth naturally. They gave me the delicate lancing device. Oh, it looked so innocuous in its cute little case, hiding its not-so-cute needle. They took me through the training of how to gently but firmly place the device on the tip of my finger and press the trigger, releasing the hidden lancet. They taught me how to gather the one drop of released blood, slide it into the glucose monitor, and watch for my numbers. They wanted me to do all this multiple times a day and jot down my numbers. They hoped to control the gestational diabetes with diet, if at all possible.

Well, I am nothing if not an executor. Not the kind with a guillotine or a noose, but the kind who learns something and tries with all her might to execute it well enough to receive a gold star. In the office, all the diabetic instruction was a piece of cake. Or a piece of kale, as the case should more properly be. What I mean is, the stabbing of oneself, the gathering of the lone droplet, and the testing of said droplet was something I had a firm grip on. I had the Big D maintenance whipped. Or so I thought.

Until I got home. Woke up the next day. And faced the necessary protocol, the taunting journal, and the pricking instrument. By myself. Somehow, on that couch, I became a bigger baby than the one I was carrying.

I can remember taking off the cap and placing the lancing device against the required finger. Ready, aim . . . Ready, aim . . . Ready, aim . . . Do not fire. Like a kid who is afraid to crank a jack-in-the-box one more turn because of the fright they know is coming. Yeah, that was me. It would have been a funny sight if it hadn't been so pitiful. I sat and I sat and I sat, poised to pull the trigger on the needle, knowing that I needed to do this very necessary, simple thing for my body so that my body could stay within healthy ranges to support new life. But I couldn't do it. For a couple of days, I actually didn't do it. I knew the risk; I understood the danger, but I just couldn't. I was stuck. (Or wasn't, as the case actually was.)

Then several friends came for a visit, and in the course of one of those visits, I told the truth on myself. I confessed that

I couldn't stab myself. I also confessed that I had missed a couple days of testing and was sort of wishful thinking my way into healthy blood sugar levels. And, much like an angel, a buddy got the implement out and sat there with me, coaching me through it. You can do it, Allison. You can do it, Allison. And—finally—I did. I pulled the trigger, braced for impact, and drew the blood. And it wasn't as awful as I thought it would be. With help, right there in my own odd desert, I began to do the extremely necessary work of caring for my body so that new life could be cared for.

A friend helped me care for myself, making certain I was getting the right kind of fuel. And as silly as my fear of the tiny pinprick was, she offered only support. Only encouragement. Just like Elijah's angel.

There is an absence of something in the whole encounter between the angel and the prophet that I think deserves a bit of holy rumination. It is the absence of the bully pulpit, the absence of the "Man of God, man up!" There is no "Pull yourself up by the sandal straps, Prophet." There isn't even a hint of accusation. Not even a strong sense of exhortation.

There is only holy comfort food, a tall drink of water, and a long snooze.

Heavenly Sleep

For he gives to his beloved sleep. (Ps. 127:2 ESV)

If I have prayed a prayer for sleep over my life once, I've prayed it a thousand times. Proclaiming. Claiming. Declaring. Begging. Bartering. Fasting. Agreeing. Waiting. I've done all I know to do and then some. I looked at that Scripture passage as some sort of shibboleth. If I could just say it clearly enough, perfectly enough, faithfully enough, then God would fulfill the passage's truth in my life.

All I wanted to do was sleep, and since adolescence, I seemed to fail at this most simple, most human of needs. Sleep was an out-of-grasp wisp. Mostly, it eluded me. Of course, there were seasons when I did sleep—or that I caught snatches of short sleep. If not, I would have died. (Yes, you can die from extreme sleep deprivation. And yes, sleep deprivation is regularly used to torture POWs. It's that formidable a weapon and that great a physical need.)

But for much of my adult life, at night I did anything but. During one difficult season, in New York, living in the pressure cooker of regularly performing in a Broadway show and regularly having to go on in different roles, I slept little to none. While I was living the performer's dream, at night I was caught in a nightmare of insomnia. I remember well the dread as I would walk home to my apartment after the show and the nightlong struggle would begin. It would often end around four or five in the morning, when my body would finally give up the ghost and collapse into some semblance of broken sleep for a little bit.

This went on for nearly twenty years. Seasons of sleeplessness followed by seasons of pseudosleep. When my mother passed away from an all-too-swift bout of pancreatic cancer, the sleeplessness returned with an ax to grind . . . and I began to despair of ever sleeping normally again. Eventually, I went to get a sleep study to see if the insomnia was as bad as I thought it was. It was. If I correctly remember the report, I slept sixty-three minutes during the hours of the sleep study, and most of those sixty-three minutes were stage 1 and 2. I never entered the third, fourth, or the deep REM sleep stage necessary for restorative sleep. I distinctly remember the nurse unwiring me in the morning and saying something along the lines of, "Ya know, most people who come in here tell us how little they sleep, and then they sleep pretty decently. You actually don't sleep much at all. And when you do, it's not very deep." With sleep apnea and other possible causes ruled out, I was left with only one culprit: the brain. The sleeplessness since adolescence was a primary symptom of pretty serious untreated and sneaky depression. Some people who struggle with depression oversleep; others undersleep. I was one of the lucky "others." Eventually, through the work of a relentless doctor and the correction of a nasty vitamin D deficiency, as well as other medicinal support, we figured out what worked for my sleep-adverse body, and I now sleep—I am happy to report—8 to 8.5 hours most nights.

All of this to say that sleep—deep, physical rest—is critical to doing just about everything, from decision making to driving. In fact, a CBS report stated this sobering bit of news: "New research shows how deadly it can be to drive when you're tired. The AAA study found drivers who miss two to three hours of sleep a day more than quadruple their risk of getting in a crash, compared to drivers who sleep for seven hours. According to federal regulators, the accident risk from drowsy driving is comparable to driving drunk."[6]

As one who lived without sleep for so long, I understand the deep importance of Elijah's sleep. The day looks quite different when you're not up all night.

And so when Elijah rose the first time to eat and drink and promptly fell back into a deep slumber, we see, apparently, that the angel waited and allowed Elijah to sleep it off.

Some of you are in a desert right now, perhaps kicking against the sandy goads, wondering how quickly you might be able to blow the joint altogether. I wonder if in your wildest heart you ever dreamed that one of the unexpected blessings God longs to bestow upon you there is a much-needed rest. A real rest.

Some of us are beyond tired. We're exhausted. The word itself comes from roots meaning "to drain off completely"— more archaically, "to drain, to draw off water."[7] Some of you are drained of all water—the very essence of survival. You're drained of anything restorative. Thinking is as thick as pea-soup fog. Simple tasks seem like running a one-legged marathon. When the alarm squawks like a shrill mockingbird, you can't recall if you slept more than half an hour. Sloths move faster than you in the a.m.—except when you're moving toward the caffeine dispenser. If so, sister, you may be suffering from exhaustion.

And as much as we think that somehow the laws of health and the way God created our bodies don't quite apply to us, they do. In fact, let us not forget that the ancient Israelites were sent into captivity, in part, for seventy years for every Sabbath year they had ignored (Lev. 26; 2 Chron. 36:21). Spiritual captivity may be awaiting us if we don't slow down.

One of my favorite Scripture passages is from Isaiah: "This is what the Sovereign LORD, the Holy One of Israel, says: 'In repentance and rest is your salvation, in quietness and trust is your strength, but you would have none of it'" (30:15). How many of us—if we are really truthful with ourselves—will have none of it? A lack of rest is such an "easy" sin to get away with because society applauds busy, active, engaged. Too often, I find that I cannot rest, if only because I have so many unique ways of staying busy. At a certain point, though, I begin to reap extremely diminished returns, running twice as hard and getting half as far. This too is the spoiled fruit of a lack of rest. The Isaiah passage goes on to warn his people ominously, saying they would continue to run, but instead of being fast, they would be overtaken by their pursuers. Now, of course, God was speaking of physical enemies and Israel's impending captivity. Remember, however, that the reason Israel's enemies could outrun them, at least partially, was because they had neglected years of rest, according to God's clear and cogent commands. How many of us also, due to a lack of rest, are galloping harder and harder, covering less and less ground, with the enemy gaining on us day by day?

I've realized, quite recently, that my lack of rest points to a deep lack in my trust in God. Though my rational mind knows better, I behave as if I believe that if I don't get something done, it won't get done. Even when God says, "It's time to turn it off today," I struggle to hit the power-down button. I forget that I am co-yoked to the One who says that his burden is easy and light, not to the one who says that his burden is grindy and nonstop. I am learning, in large part due to the ministry of the desert, the truth of this passage: "Return to your rest, my soul, for the LORD has been good to you" (Ps. 116:7).

Yes, soul, return to your desert rest. Sometimes a girl, just like the power prophet, has to take a spiritual power nap. And when she wakes up, she may have to rinse, wash, and repeat. She may have to do it all over again until the tank begins to fill up.

Heavenly Rhythms

Notice how Elijah ate and drank after the angelic touch and then "lay down again" (1 Kings 19:6). And the passage continues, as it paints a most loving, almost parental picture, with, "And the angel of the LORD came again a second time and touched him and said, 'Arise and eat, for the journey is too great for you'" (v. 7 ESV).

Aside from the fact that the angel touched him again and fed him again, in effect saying that their work was not quite finished, it is the next words of the Lord's angel that touch something deep inside me—something I struggle to articulate.

This journey is too much for you. The angel, with great kindness, says that the journey you still need to take is too much for you.

Jesus knows when what is coming will take more strength than we have at the moment. Jesus knows when the fuel on which we are running will not get us across the finish line. Jesus knows—sister, he knows—when the journey ahead will exact from us a price we cannot pay. He knows. And he knows if we need to eat, drink, sleep a second time. Or a tenth. Or a hundredth.

Perhaps you need to sit for a moment and hear the care of Jesus for you: "This journey is still too much for you. Daughter, we have to fill you up so you can be sent out."

My greatest prayer is that you would listen to him and the messengers he sends. Jesus is trustworthy with the rhythms of your life, even when those rhythms seem simple.

Eat. Drink. Sleep. Repeat.

Please know that the journey doesn't end with you and me (and the prophet Elijah) exhausted and exiled under a broom tree. There is still a journey to take. After we have surrendered to the desert blessing of rest and restoration, then we can finally stand back up, get our desert legs back underneath us, and start that journey. Just like Elijah.

In the desert, God has done business with the body. And now he can do business with the soul.

Which is what comes next.

Reflections

An old man came into Abba John's cell and found him asleep, with an angel standing over him, fanning him. Seeing this, he withdrew.[8]

Have you ever needed a deep sleep? A deep season of rest? How do you think Jesus might use a quiet desert season to accomplish this in your life? Do you run from or run to rest? How have you built regular rhythms of rest into your life? If you haven't, how might you do so?

7

Revelation

A brother said to Abba Poemen, "Give me a word . . ."

The Sayings of the Desert Fathers[1]

The voice of the Lord shakes the desert, the Lord shakes the Desert of Kadesh.

Psalm 29:8 Oxford NIV

And he [Elijah] arose and ate and drank, and went in the strength of that food forty days and forty nights to Horeb, the mount of God.

1 Kings 19:8 ESV

*A*fter Elijah rested and ate and drank and repeated, going in the "strength of that food," he began his long journey to Mount Horeb, the mountain of God. Sometimes called Mount Horeb and sometimes called Mount

Horeb and sometimes called Mount Sinai, this was the mountainous outcropping where the revelation of the law was first given to and through Moses.[2] Moses, another desert tenant we will encounter, heard the audible voice of God near this mountain and years later received God's revealed law there.

Elijah knew all of this as he began the sandy journey after the ministry of the angelic visitor. He knew that Horeb/Sinai was a place where God had acted as the great Revealer, unveiling his will in the most unusual, explosive ways.

Elijah was going up to the mount of God to meet with God. Elijah was going up to gain revelation.

Forty

We know little about his forty-day and forty-night journey to the mount of God, but in the Bible, forty represents completeness. The children of Israel wandered for forty years. It rained for forty days and nights while the ark floated. Jesus's desert battle waged for forty days and nights, the same length of time as Elijah's trip to Horeb.

We know when Elijah departed for Horeb, and we know what happened when he arrived, but I cannot help wondering about his sojourn. I cannot help but wonder what happened during those forty days. I wonder if Elijah walked in absolute quiet, steeling himself for difficult step after difficult step. I wonder how much he slept. I wonder what he thought about. I wonder if, as he trudged forward, he replayed his confusing, painful cry for death under the broom tree. I wonder if unbidden images of Ahab and Jezebel and the doomed prophets of Ba'al tramped around his brain. I wonder if he made a list of pros and cons regarding his ministry, contemplating whether

110

he should continue with the whole prophet thing. The Bible is mum about Elijah's internal dialogue with God in the forty-day journey through the hostile landscape. We only know what happened when he arrived at God's mountain, but I believe that Elijah's first words give us some sense of where he had been spiritually for the last forty days and nights:

> There he came to a cave and lodged in it. And behold, the word of the LORD came to him, and he said to him, "What are you doing here, Elijah?" He said, "I have been very jealous for the LORD, the God of hosts. For the people of Israel have forsaken your covenant, thrown down your altars, and killed your prophets with the sword, and I, even I only, am left, and they seek my life, to take it away." And he said, "Go out and stand on the mount before the LORD." (1 Kings 19:9–11 ESV)

Questions in the Bible have tremendous power. The first question of Genesis is a powerhouse: Where are you, Adam? And a similar ring exists in this interrogative to Elijah: What are you doing here? We know that God was not confused about Adam's physical locale when he asked Adam, "Where are you?" any more than he was unaware of what Elijah was doing tucked away in a cave when he asked the prophet, "What are you doing here?"

There is a common theme in both instances, and it has to do with the first peg of our desert tent.

Back to Peg One

Remember those tent pegs?

heart revelation

heart restoration

heart release

Well, that first peg—heart revelation—was being driven deep into the sand in Elijah's desert. And God was using a question to get at it.

What are you doing here, Elijah?

Elijah said, "I have been very jealous for the Lord, the God of hosts. For the people of Israel have forsaken your covenant, thrown down your altars, and killed your prophets with the sword, and I, even I only, am left, and they seek my life, to take it away" (1 Kings 19:10 ESV).

I don't know about you, but when I read Elijah's words, I see something else at work, something actors like to call subtext—the real meaning or intention underneath (sub) the words (text) we are saying. In a show, an actor might be tasked to say the text, "I love you," but the subtext might be, "I love you so much *that I'm about to do something stupid.*" Or "I love you. *Please don't ever leave me.*" One is text. The other is subtext. I think something similar was going on with the prophet at this moment. Elijah carefully recounted his ministry and the reaction to his ministry:

> I am jealous and zealous for you, the One who commands the angelic hosts. Your people, the children of Israel, have trampled on your covenant, kicked down your altars, and run your holy men through with the sword. And I am the only one left standing for you and for righteousness, and now they want me too. (1 Kings 19:10, paraphrased)

That was Elijah's text.

But I think he also had a subtext working, and I think that subtext was something like this: "Um, God, I've done everything you said to do. Fought every battle you asked me to. And I am alone in this ordeal. I don't feel like anyone is standing with me. I feel so alone. And now Jezebel is coming for my life." Don't you hear Elijah telling the truth on himself, his subtext fairly screaming, "I didn't think the story of my life was going to end this way. I thought life was supposed to go more favorably for someone who has been so gung ho for your name. I thought there would be more covering, more like-minded company, more goodness. More of your obvious hand. I did not think life serving you was going to be this hard."

If we are honest, many of us have thought something along these lines. The audacious thing is that God cared about the contents of Elijah's heart. God cared about his feelings.

Aw, feelings.

For much of my early Christian sojourn, I had a tendency that I mistakenly believed was a holy one. I put my feelings in a bottle, corked it, and separated them from the rest of me. I would think very pseudospiritual-sounding things like, *Look here, emotions, bottle it up until you are ready to allow the rational part to take the lead.*

Now, please hear me. I am not saying that we need to live our lives driven by emotion, nor am I saying that emotions should run roughshod over good choices or godly behavior. I'm not even saying that hitting the pause button on wild emotions so wisdom can win is the smart chick's best choice. I'm saying that, on the whole, I had developed a strange complex about my emotions—a strange way of categorizing them. They were lesser than. I relegated them to the unredeemable, unusable column in my mind. I discounted my feelings, like many of us discount the physical body. I parsed myself; I chopped myself up—as if feelings were a two-headed monster lurking in the basement. Best to keep them locked up. And out of sight.

As if God would ever want this. As if he is more interested in our will than our feelings. As if our thinking is more important than our tears.

I've been coming to a slow revelation—over the course of many years and through many healing conversations—that God is a "wholistic" God, in that he comes for and delights in and redeems us entirely, the whole of our beings. In addition, I'm coming to the realization that our feelings are God given and, as such, are beautiful and useful. When I feel agony, when I tear up over the despicable fact that twenty-seven million made-in-the-image-of-God people are enslaved in our modern, justice-aware world, my raw emotion moves me to action. Jesus wept when he heard of Lazarus's death. Jesus wept over Jerusalem. Jesus was moved with compassion—literally "moved in the in-ward parts"[3]—toward widows and lepers and mothers bereft of children and sisters bereft of brothers. Jesus felt, and being made in his image means that we are free to feel. And we should celebrate the feeling parts of us. He never asks me to split off parts of myself in an effort to hide them from his hand and heart. He doesn't ask that of you. And he didn't ask it of Elijah.

Speaking of which.

God didn't want to hear what Elijah *thought* should be in his heart or *wanted* to be in his heart or *knew* should be in his heart. God wanted to know what was really there. He wanted to know what Elijah truly felt. And more truly, he wanted Elijah to know. God wanted to reveal Elijah's heart back to him there in the desert.

I Expected . . .

When I was a twentysomething believer, I waded through a particularly disorienting relational season—one that had taken me by surprise—also, one that I couldn't seem to get a handle on. A particular conversation during that time was paradigm-shifting for me, in that it revealed an issue that could be at the root of relationship tension. My pastor at the time, Terry Sartain, enlightened me that in his many years counseling troubled relationships, he had discovered that much of the struggle sprang from expectations—often never expressed. Expectation is a strong belief that something *will* happen or *will* be the case in the future, and Terry told me that when we carry these expectations around in our hearts without expressing them, they can do untold damage to relational health. How true. I've seen that played out in my human relationships, and I see it played out in technicolor in Elijah's relationship with God.

Into the desert, Elijah is carrying the heart-crippling burden of unexpressed and, I would add, unsanctified expectations. It's like Elijah was saying, "I expected life to be a little bit rosier for one of your servants. I expected not to have to go solo up the mountain. I expected . . . I expected . . ." Oh, the power of unsanctified expectations.

We see this played out in Elijah's answer. "I've been zealous for you, and that should have meant something. Things should have ended up differently. I shouldn't have a crazy woman coming after my head." A + B should equal C. A + B should not equal Z. The future should have looked predictably different. Elijah was deeply disappointed in the outcome of serving God in this specific case. And the reason his expectations were unsanctified, in my humble opinion, is that perhaps they were not rooted in God in the first place. God never promised Elijah that the road would be easy or that someone would never want him six feet under the sand. When Elijah went into a diatribe about his own unfair treatment, Elijah didn't realize that spiritual entitlement—unsanctified expectations rather than sanctified hope—had infected his heart. For Elijah and for us, it often takes the desert to deliver us to the revealed truth of what lies within.

Let's talk about those things, Elijah. Let's talk about those things, desert walker.

Have you ever carted around unsanctified expectations? Things that have become almost demands? Almost foregone conclusions? Almost scarily near to entitlements? Regarding ministry. Regarding God himself. Have you ever put your hope in an outcome rather than in the Lord of the outcome? Boy, I've been there before, looking to God for his revelation only to discover that he was looking to reveal me.

If our hearts are full of that mangled material, we must allow the gentle proddings of God to reveal our false expectations. Remember that the Bible says, "God led you all the way in the wilderness . . . to humble and test you in order to know what was in your heart" (Deut. 8:2).

Oh, the revelation of God, plumbing the depths we think no one could ever plumb.

What Lurks Within

Once, as a kid in North Carolina, I was invited to go swimming in a quarry outside the city I lived in. The quarry was cavernous, frigid, impenetrable, and quite able to take your life, if the urban legend my friend told me was to be believed. Apparently, an unnamed senior (the unnamed part never would have passed Snopes muster, but this was the eighties, and urban myths were our version of the internet gone awry) "years" before had jumped from the cliffs into the waters below. He came up long enough to yell, "Don't jump!" to his friends, watching horrified on the cliffs' edges. Apparently, he had dived into a nest of water moccasins. The story didn't end well for the unnamed senior, or so went the legend I remember.

I remembered thinking about the terrifying story as I prepared to jump into the opaque hole of water. What I recall more than the sudden shock of cold that overtook me as I sliced the cold hole of water was my inability to see even the faintest outline of my arms and legs. That, as well as my inability to touch the bottom, made me want to exit posthaste. I'm sure I made some excuse to my friends to get out of the quarry water that day. Probably something innocuous like, "I wanna get some sun." The rocks I had to climb to make an exit were slick with something like moss, and I slipped on one, cutting my leg and sliding back into the giant, gaping hole. I'd heard that there were cars and buses at the bottom of our North Carolina rock quarry, but now I imagined great whites and giant squid and other unspeakable evils in the gray-green murk. By sheer will, I heaved my dripping body weight over my forearms, threw my rump on a rock, and looked back for strange ripples in the water, wondering what was underneath.

Though a real-life experience, my quarry swim morphed into something of a living parable for my own heart. I remember, looking back on that scary swim, that the concern about what lay underneath—what I could not see—was what stayed with me long after the dip in the murky waters had taken place.

In some ways, for years, I carried something like that quarry inside my heart—until I sat on a couch and entered into a three-month desert that began to dry up those murky waters and reveal the things lying on the deepest floor.

Waving the Flag

I'm not sure what week the waterline started to lower on the walls of my heart. I only know that as I sat—unable to move, unable to do anything, unable to be able—I started to answer a version of God's question to Elijah.

What are you doing here?

And that question had the ability to dive down to the bottom floor of the quarry to things I thought no one saw. But, of course, God saw. God always saw.

I'm going to see if I can creatively re-create some of the conversations and prayer times I shared with God during those dog days of summer.

What are you doing here, Allison?

Well, Lord, I'm here because my cervix is faulty and there is a real danger I might lose this miracle babe if the cerclage doesn't hold. Technically, that's why I'm here, on this couch.

What are you doing here, Allison?

Well, respectfully, Lord, I've tried to answer that question, but if you're asking what I'm feeling while I'm here, I can give that a whirl. Emotionally, I am a tangled-up necklace.

I guess I thought bed rest would play out a little differently. Somehow.

I mean this to the core: your people, as a whole, have been incredible. Sustaining, generous, surprisingly good. The picture of the body has been a masterpiece. We have wanted for nothing. Not a meal. Not a carpool need. Nothing.

So please allow me to say that though my rational mind knows that truth, my heart says something else.

While the body has operated with stunning efficiency, I thought—more rightly stated, expected—that others would be more a part of this process, would come closer in. But some of the closest have not come closest, and this has surprised me. Thrown me off-kilter.

I find myself weighing the weight of relationships. Perhaps certain ones mean more to me than they should. I have been forced to redefine that which I never thought I would redefine.

Hard to say. Harder to feel.

And then there's Mom. Mom.

Mostly, I can get through a day without that surfacing, until this couch.

Mom came alive in a way I had never seen when she became a grandmother to Levi. And for her to depart just as he turned eighteen months—to have her back fully alive for such a short time, for weeks really—well, Lord, my words are too petite for it. The animalistic agony. Living with absence. Living without presence. Even six years later, time without her feels like both thirty minutes and thirty years.

And when she got sick, I was unprepared for your answer to be no. I expected something different. I had participated in many great yeses in the kingdom; I expected one too. But it was no. No, I will not be healing her on this side of eternity, Allison.

Instead, I will witness her writhing and itching, until I give the hospice nurse the okay to run her through with morphine, and as they do so, she will look at me and say these last words: "I love you." In the end, love after all. I will stand over her as she moves her lips as if she still has something to say, as if she wants to hold on to this short life, and I'll say the simplest of things: *I'm here. I love you. We're here. We love you.*

And then near the end, when the breathing rattles, I will pick flowers—her mother's petunias—from her mother's land, not sure if she can still smell. And I will lay them by her bed, in her sister's house. And the music will play: choruses, hymns, flights of angels singing her to her rest.

And at the end, the begging, the pleading for you to take her fast. And this prayer you will answer. Even the hospice nurses will be surprised at how fast her feet and hands go cold, explaining over the phone as dusk falls, in sweet, gentling tones, that it will not be long. Stay close. Stay close when the hands go cold. Stay close when the panting begins. And she will wait until my brother walks into my aunt's house—somehow she senses he is there—and I will run and yell after him, "She's going, Jim! She's going, Jim!" And she will give up the ghost between a trinity of people—my brother, her sister, and me.

You were in every minute of it, and I saw you there. I saw goodness and hope, like a few rare gems in an ash heap. I know death is swallowed up in life for all eternity, but I wanted it to be slower. I wanted eternity's appetite to slow down.

And now, I am pregnant again with a child that, if we make it through this desert, she will never see. Sure, some people I thought would come close didn't, but underneath all that was one person—Mom—I wanted closer than anyone else. And that is an impossibility.

Did you cringe at some of those words when you read them? I did when I wrote some of them, blurry eyed with tears, even years later. Raw. Discordant. Painful. Experienced as very True.

So much harder than the intense communion with the couch was the intense communion with the contents of my heart—a heart that was full to the brim with unsanctified expectations of people and unexpressed pain regarding my mother. Expectations. Unsanctified, unexpressed. The way I had hoped (let's get real, *expected*) the whole experience of having a miracle baby—of life in general—would play out as a child of God.

And Finally Comes the Response

I wasn't in a cave like Elijah, but, like Elijah, I was hiding out, and when God gave me my own version of "Go out and stand on the mount before the Lord," I did. Like Elijah, I didn't find God in fireworks and earthquakes, in signs and wonders and magical answers to prayers about turning back the clock, stopping up the skies, or raising the dead. I found him, as Elijah did, in the still, small voice that spoke after such natural fireworks.

To Elijah's cry of entitlement, "I have been very zealous for the Lord . . . they have tried to kill me . . . and now, I am the only one left," God finally answered. The Lord of the Outcome spoke:

> When you say, "I, even I only, am left," it is not so. Others are waiting in the wings, handpicked for the next stage of ministry. So here are the next steps. Here is your answer: Go anoint Elisha as prophet. Go anoint Hazael over Syria. Go anoint Jehu as king of Israel. Go use your gift to raise up the next generation of leaders. And, by the way, I have reserved seven thousand people for myself who have not bowed down and worshiped Baal or kissed him on the lips. When you think you are alone, Elijah, think again.

My own response from God was something simpler. No specific directives. No grand insights into the kingdom. God gave me two sets of three words. One we talked about in the first chapter: wave the flag. The other, in danger of forever being identified with princesses and ice, was let it go.

The Father whispered . . .

Wave the flag.

Let it go.

I sat with it and realized so much. The things I felt entitled to, the things I expected, weren't helping me; they were handicapping me. Jesus wanted to take me places, and those things couldn't ride shotgun any longer. The outcomes I so desperately wanted to control were never in my job description. The things that hurt me and drove me had the ability to do so because I had a misplaced hope. In things Jesus never promised me. In relationship outcomes he never promised me. He promised me himself, and the thousand good things that entailed, but he never promised that death wouldn't touch me. He never promised that people wouldn't disappoint me, any more than he promised that I wouldn't disappoint others. I had to let the weight of unsanctified expectations go so that I could be free to move into a new season with him. Let it go. Wave the flag.

As crazy as it may seem, I remember emailing myself Jesus's "let it go/wave the flag" message the very next day. And several more times on my desert couch. I had to remind myself of the desert lesson over and over again until my heart took its first tentative steps toward believing it.

Was letting go easy? No. In fact, it was one of the hardest things I have ever done in my life. To let go of people and still love them? To let go of outcomes and trust Jesus, no matter the outcomes? Excruciating and absolutely necessary. Letting go just may be the bravest thing you ever do, because what waits on the other side of letting go is often a mystery. And is never guaranteed. We don't know what happens on the other side of letting go, but we do know that, because Jesus is there, it is always and ever for our good.

Friend, if you find yourself waylaid in a desert, and in that desert you hear the still, small voice of God telling you to let some old things go, rejoice. The still, small voice of God reveals the heart, changing everything.

The voice of the Lord shakes the desert.

And the heart that resides within it.

Reflections

Teach your mouth to say that which you have in your heart.

Poemen, desert father[4]

Do you feel entitled to certain things—even in the kingdom? Perhaps especially in the kingdom? Do you feel like Elijah and need to have an encounter that reveals your heart? Do unsanctified and unexpressed expectations reside there? What would you say to God in an unfiltered way?

8

Intimacy

Search me, God, and know my heart. . . .
See if there is any offensive way in me,
and lead me in the way everlasting.

Psalm 139:23–24

If a man does not say in his heart, in the world there is
only myself and God, he will not gain peace.

Alonius, desert father[1]

Therefore I am now going to allure her;
I will lead her into the desert
and speak tenderly to her.
There I will give her back her vineyards,
and will make the Valley of Achor a doorway of hope.

There she will sing as in the days of her youth,
　　as in the day she came up out of Egypt.
"In that day," declares the LORD,
　　"you will call me 'my husband';
　　you will no longer call me 'my master.'
I will remove the names of the Baals from her lips;
　　no longer will their names be invoked.
In that day I will make a covenant for them,
　　with the beasts of the field and the birds of the air
　　and the creatures that move along the ground.
Bow and sword and battle
　　I will abolish from the land,
　　so that all may lie down in safety.
I will betroth you to me forever;
　　I will betroth you in righteousness and justice,
　　in love and compassion.
I will betroth you in faithfulness,
　　and you will acknowledge the LORD." (Hos. 2:14–20
　　Oxford NIV)

There are unexpected, uncountable blessings to be found in our dry and difficult desert seasons—blessings that we can ultimately take with us when the seasons are over—when we live out those trying circumstances unto and under the grace of Christ. In his hands, the most ominous and obliterating periods of difficulty often yield gifts that come to us in few other ways. We've looked at the first tent peg—how God reveals the heart—with the heart revelation of Elijah's story. God doesn't stop there, though. He hammers the second tent peg down deep (restoration)—ultimately striking one of the rarest desert diamonds—the gem of intimacy.

And true intimacy can restore our hearts like little else.

One of the greatest definitions of intimacy that I have heard is into-me-see. True intimacy exists at a level of transparency that is hard to articulate. Too deep for explaining. All is laid bare, exposed, laid open. What lies beneath surfaces. Wonder and warts. Willingness and waywardness. Wounding and wonder. Nothing is hidden. All known. All seen.

This intimate state is deeply reflected in one of my favorite psalms, Psalm 139, written by David. Even the subtitle of the psalm has intimate overtones: "To the choirmaster. A Psalm of David." Of David. It might as well be entitled "A Psalm of Intimacy," for the intimate, knowing words David chooses. The cry of the heart to be known by God is tender, rare. It's a cry to be seen in the secret place, to the very core where human eyes cannot peer. At least not as deeply as God's.

This is how David renders the intimate encounter.

> O LORD, you have searched me and known me!
> You know when I sit down and when I rise up;
>   you discern my thoughts from afar.
> You search out my path and my lying down
>   and are acquainted with all my ways.
> Even before a word is on my tongue,
>   behold, O LORD, you know it altogether.
> You hem me in, behind and before,
>   and lay your hand upon me.
> Such knowledge is too wonderful for me;
>   it is high; I cannot contain it.
> Where shall I go from your Spirit?
>   Or where shall I flee from your presence?
> If I ascend to heaven, you are there!
>   If I make my bed in Sheol, you are there!

If I take the wings of the morning
and dwell in the uttermost parts of the sea,
even there your hand shall lead me,
and your right hand shall hold me. . . .
How precious to me are your thoughts, O God!
How vast is the sum of them!
If I would count them, they are more than the sand.
I awake, and I am still with you. . . .
Search me, O God, and know my heart!
Try me and know my thoughts!
And see if there be any grievous way in me,
and lead me in the way everlasting. (vv. 1–10, 17–18,
23–24 ESV)

Search me. Know me. Discern my thoughts. Hem me in. Lay your hand on me. The final high point of David's intimate cry concludes with, "Search me, O God, and know my heart! Try me and know my thoughts! And see if there be any grievous way in me, and lead me in the way everlasting" (vv. 23–24 ESV).

Early on in my Christian walk, Psalm 139 was my favorite psalm—I even composed a song about it with the looping chorus, "Lead me in the everlasting way now." I wanted it so much that I wrote about it. I've often found that in my own life, I write what I most need to learn. Despite my passionate lyric, the truth of the matter was that there always seemed to be an opaque veil between me and God. It was thin, to be sure, but remained cloudy.

I likened myself to the man in Matthew 12 who had to stretch out his withered hand—likely the thing he had kept hidden for so long—for Jesus to heal it. There was so much I thought I had hidden away from him, because I had hidden so much away from myself. I didn't understand that he already saw, knew, understood. I was like a young kid playing hide-and-seek, face buried in hands, while the child's amused parents are already in the room, thinking, *How cute that she thinks we can't see her.* Something amazing happens when we allow ourselves to experience the deep intimacy of God in Christ—a gift that is always ours, always at the ready, always available.

Look back at that gorgeous, intimate, Hosea passage at the beginning of the chapter for just a moment. Among the incredible blessings and beautiful gifts God gives in this particular desert passage (and there are many) is the gift of intimacy. The language is so tender. So knowing. In fact, the entire desert experience finishes with a betrothal. Between God and Israel. Between God and the hearts of his people. He promises that what is to come is the deepest of intimacies, found in the most intimate of relationships: marriage. Years back, I discovered that Hosea's use of the word *betrothal* can mean "to woo a virgin,"[2] a pure, untouched woman. This is full of dramatic, redemptive irony, if you know anything about Hosea, the man who penned such surprising words, and his story.

Hosea and the Desert

We know little of Hosea outside the book that bears his name. We don't know his occupation, though many scholars think he might have been a farmer, due to the abundance of agricultural references in his book. I like this man. Hosea reminds me of the people from whom I hail in South Carolina. I wonder if, like many in agricultural communities, Hosea had caked dirt on his work boots. If he loved to run his hands through the soil. If he could plant and coax and fix and build. Whoever Hosea was and whatever exactly Hosea did, we can be fairly certain he did not have any idea what kind of dust storm was headed his way. Check out how quickly foul weather descended:

> The word of the LORD that came to Hosea son of Beeri during the reigns of Uzziah, Jotham, Ahaz and Hezekiah, kings of Judah, and during the reign of Jeroboam son of Jehoash king of Israel:
> When the LORD began to speak through Hosea, the LORD said to him, "Go, marry a promiscuous woman and have children with her, for like an adulterous wife this land is guilty of unfaithfulness to the LORD." So he married Gomer daughter of Diblaim, and she conceived and bore him a son. (Hos. 1:1–3)

In verse 2, Hosea's life took a massive detour. God commanded Hosea to take an adulterous wife and bear children with her, because the land had become the personification of a cheating woman, guilty of flagrant and vile adultery against God himself. Hosea, the prophet, was to enter into a living object lesson for the entire nation of Israel. The Bible records that his acquiescence was immediate. He married the girl with the odd name, and they were fruitful and multiplied.

God commanded Hosea, "Take an adulterous wife [or one who will yet be adulterous, according to some thinkers]. Go do it, but I want you to know what's coming, Hosea. I am forewarning you, Prophet. The story will not be a pretty one. She will look ravishing in the veil. She will swear to give you her heart and her body exclusively, but I tell you that she will shred your soul, she will be with other men, she will bear children not of your own loins. You will name them and raise them and feed them as if they were your own flesh and bone. This you will do to show and warn my people of my call to return and impending judgment and captivity if they do not return to me."

We can never say that God isn't long-suffering. Hosea had one of the longest prophetic tenures in all of the Bible, as many as three-plus decades according to some calculations. But I digress. Let us get back to God's warning to Hosea about his marriage to Gomer.

"Gomer will not stop at adultery and having children with other men. She will run off. She will shack up with her lovers, reflecting the incredible sexual perversion my people dally with daily. And you, Hosea, as a representation of my heart for my people, will go and buy her back for fifteen shekels and a measure of barley, about half price for a slave. You, Hosea, will bring her home. After a soul sabbatical, during which Gomer will rest and reflect, she will be restored—restored to you, Hosea, as her rightful husband.

"And through all of it, Prophet, though I prophesy to you a shredded heart and a shamed marital bed, you will love her anyway. You will chase Gomer anyway. You will rescue Gomer anyway. You will redeem Gomer anyway. Just like me. Just like my heart toward my people."

When God first called Israel out of Egypt, she came faithfully (perhaps like Gomer at her wedding to Hosea). God even says so in Jeremiah 2:2: "This is what the LORD says: 'I remember the devotion of your youth, how as a bride you loved me and followed me through the wilderness [desert], through a land not sown.'" Oh, Israel—Oh, Gomer—how beautiful, how tender our love was at first. How faithfully and innocently you followed me through a land not sown. Through the wilderness. Through the desert. And then, degree by degree, drip by drip, choice by choice, everything fell into chaos.

But chaos doesn't win the day. God says, after a long spiritual season, after rest and quiet, allured into the desert once again, you will return to a state of intimacy with me. Because returning you to intimacy and to my intimate heart has always been the end game.

But to do that, a very big Goliath needs to be dealt with: idolatry.

An Idol Heart?

My personal definition of idolatry is anything that usurps God's rightful and primary place in our hearts and lives. It's no different than what an illicit affair would do to a spouse. Idolatry leads us down a million dead-end and destructive paths, but for the ancient Israelites, it did all that and more. Idolatry blocked and skewed intimacy with almighty God. In fact, this was one of the main reasons he allured wayward Israel into the desert—to deal with her deep-seated idolatry.

In our wellspring Scripture passage, in verse 17, God says, "I will remove the names of the Baals from her lips." Here, "Baal" is a name for a Canaanite god who controlled many aspects of life, especially weather and rain. The symbolism is complex, but suffice it to say that in agrarian societies, survival was rooted to the land and, hence, the weather.[3] The ESV Study Bible boils it down perfectly: "Since the ancient Israel was always an agricultural society, Baal worship was of unrivaled importance."[4] Worship of Baal or baals often included strange fertility rights, as well as temple prostitution and all manner of sexual antics.[5] When Gomer descended into a life of sexual adultery and prostitution, she was mirroring Israel's decline into idolatry in her own living flesh. I have often wondered if it might be possible that Gomer had become a temple prostitute, a common practice in Baal worship. Whatever the case, the idolatry of Baal had been woven into the very fabric of Israel's life.

Interestingly, the Israelites didn't kick their worship of Yahweh to the curb altogether during this period. They just added a dash of Baal worship to it, acting as if the fertility god could be a cute little side dish to Israel's main entrée of God himself. Again, the ESV Study Bible paints a poignant picture: "The Israelites had fused the name of the Lord with Baal, as though doing so made no difference."[6]

In other words, Israel had a major usurper in her heart. There was an area in which they did not trust God to be God—their everyday life concerns of rain and children and crops. And this lack of trust—this idolatry—was ultimately revealed on her lips. Look again at the Scripture passage. It says, "I will remove the names of the Baals *from her lips*; no longer will their names be invoked" (Hos. 2:17). This is an obvious reference to worship—and intoning the name of Baal in some twisted form of prayer—but I find another interesting tidbit here in the passage. Our idols, no differently than Israel's, are exposed by our lips one idolatrous word at a time. What consumes our thoughts will come forth from our mouths. Jesus said, "For the mouth speaks what the heart is full of" (Luke 6:45). Our words, Jesus said, are evidence of anything (including idolatry) that has consumed our hearts.

In our desert wellspring Scripture passage, God is saying, through the prophet Hosea, I'm going to remove the evidence of your idol's brutal residency in your life, and the way to do that is to deal with the root of the problem—which resides in your heart. Because your heart is divided, you speak out of both sides of your mouth, one side for Yahweh and another side for Baal. When your heart is singular—when

133

Baal idolatry has been rooted out—then your lips will reflect truth.

Remember that, very often, the desert is all about the heart of the matter and the matter of the heart. In my own life, when I get a sneaking suspicion that I may have a lurking idol— something that has usurped God's rightful place—I have to look no farther than my own mouth, which leads me no farther than my own heart, a heart that God is longing to restore, sometimes in the most unusual of ways.

Final Funerals

In verse 15 of Hosea 2, God says these words: "I . . . will make the Valley of Achor a doorway of hope." When I first studied the passage years ago, I thought this was some poetically obscure reference to some ancient place, which it is, but it is that and so much more. It was a place where, in terrible technicolor, God restored the nation after a serious encounter with secret idolatry. God used that ancient valley to do business with his people and their "idol" hearts. The word *Achor* means "trouble," and in that particular desert valley, God came against something that had troubled Israel for a very long time. Her idols.

As we venture down into the desert Valley of Achor, we have to think about two other *A* words: the person of Achan and the Canaanite city of Ai. Let's first throw the spotlight on our leading man, Achan.

Achan was a pedigreed Israelite and a fighter who, when taking the city of Ai during ancient Israel's conquest of the Promised Land, kept some of the fallen city's spoils (or the devoted/accursed things) and hid them underneath his tent. He took a specific garment and a large amount of gold and silver.

This theft was a blatant slap in the face to God; the devoted things were never to be taken and placed among one's personal belongings. These stolen goods acted as functional idols in Achan's life—cursed objects that made him arrogantly defy the preeminence of God, not to mention God's commands— and were the impetus for one of the most vehement and vigorous judgments God ever meted out in the entirety of Scripture.

Tragically, because Achan had taken some of the accursed things of Ai, the Valley of Achor would be the final resting place of Achan and his family. His funeral—and the funeral of many he loved—would occur right there. In the Valley of Achor, Achan, his children, and his livestock were stoned by the nation of Israel.

To be frank, I wince when reading this account in Joshua 7. I have a hard time stomaching the perishing of family members for what appears to be the sin of someone else. Scholars point out that the nation of Israel was seen as a whole to God, much like the body of Christ is today.[7] And they further state that the idolatrous effect of Canaanite worship had to be cut off like the cancer it was. Hard as it is to swallow, this bloody judgment was akin to cutting off a gangrenous limb so that the entire body doesn't succumb to the infection, a terrible medicine for an absolutely necessary cure. Under the old covenant, Achan's sin—and his family line—had to be rooted out, lest the whole field be spoiled with thistles.[8]

Tragically, the people of Israel were instructed to take Achan, his family, and all that was his to the Valley of Achor and then stone them and burn the remains. Typing that was hard. Living it must have been excruciating, especially since the nation itself had to execute the verdict. They had to pick up the desert stones, circle the victims, and fire away.

God was deathly serious about the people of God keeping the first of the Ten Commandments of God: "You shall have no other gods before me" (Exod. 20:3).

Considering the brutality of God's judgment on Achan and his family and the fact that the Israelites themselves had to participate in the exacting of that justice, it is comforting to note that the passage from Hosea doesn't stop with the Valley of Achor. God could have left them at the place of judgment and "trouble," leaving the scene as a morality tale for the people of the northern kingdom, to whom Hosea was specifically writing. But he didn't. God moved from "trouble" to "hope." God finished the passage with, "I . . . will make the Valley of Achor a door of hope" (2:15).

This makes my mouth fall open like that of a teenaged girl at a K-pop concert. God was promising that what was once the valley of trouble, a place of exacting judgment and unthinkable bloodshed, would somehow, in his hands, become a door of hope. And he added a key phrase: I will do it. *I* will transform it. *I* will make trouble, hope. *I* will make valleys, doors. In me, a stuck place will become a passageway to somewhere else.

But between those two points is a funeral of sorts.

My Own Valley of Achor

To you, it would have looked like a normal leather couch. It was new, so there weren't yet the scratches and nicks and rubbings that eventually come to mark all such leather furniture. Maybe an indentation in the cushioning where my burgeoning self sat, maybe a happy tearstain from when my little Levi, one day while heading out for school, called me Jabba the Hutt. Oh, the indignities of diabetic pregnancy, plenteous casseroles, and the ability to exercise not a whit. I admit, we howled at the reference we were certain showed his brilliance (if not a penchant for things Star Wars-ian) and still regularly speak of this welcome, verbal bright spot in the difficult dryness of the desert experience on the couch.

But in God's hands, that couch became my own Valley of Achor. Somewhere in the three-month desert stint, I felt God whisper, *Allison, we're on the move. Internally. We are on the move into a wilderness valley called Achor.*

As we traveled down, I had the distinct sense that I had the same monkey on my back as Achan and the people of Israel. I, too, had taken some "accursed" things. I, too, was in trouble and troubled. I, too, possessed an idolatrous heart.

My idols were not little dancing fertility figurines wrapped in precious gems and metals. I like to think had they been so corporeal, so concrete, I would have spotted them setting up shop years earlier and chopped them up the minute they reared their idolatrous, usurping heads. But modern idols are not so conspicuous. At least not for me.

My idols came wrapped not in gold and emerald but in flesh and blood. More accurately, in the flesh and blood of other people—other dear people I loved, who meant the emotional world to me, whom I had built the relational scaffolding of my life around. That's how I would have explained some of my friendships to you.

But underneath all that care and concern and closeness lay another reality. In truth, beyond simply befriending some of them, I had come near to worshiping some of them. Emotionally, they consumed me. They took heart space and mind space and time space that was God's and God's alone. Friends, I tell you, without the desert, this is a reality—an idolatrous reality—I do not believe I would have ever identified. And I believe it would have stunted me, perhaps for a very long time. Perhaps for life.

Because my idols came with middle names and memorized cell numbers, and because I had a lengthy and rich history with them, I couldn't easily identify them as idols in my life. No one ever thinks something so ostensibly good could produce not-so-good fruit in one's life. I never realized that meandering through my mind almost any time I stopped long enough to tune in were thoughts like, "I wonder what [insert names] would think," or "I wonder how [insert names] would feel," or "I wonder what [insert names] are doing," or "I wonder what [insert names] would think about what I am doing." I think you get the picture.

The people I idolized never demanded such idolization from me. Consuming attention was not a prerequisite to relationship with them. Not in any way. In fact, to this day, they may be largely unaware of the primary position they had taken up in my life. They didn't ask to sit on the throne—not once. For a long time, I had no idea they were standing on the gold medalist's stand while Jesus was taking home the silver, maybe even the bronze. The whole thing had snuck up on me, this relational idolatry. My heart was listing like an off-balance ship taking on water, and God wanted to right it again.

The whole experience was hard to pin down and even harder to push through. So when God nudged, *Let's take it all down into the Valley of Achor,* and I got the first hint of what he was getting at, I thought I might shake apart like an ill-balanced washing machine. The weight was lopsided, too heavy, the cost too untenable, the loss too staggering. I knew a funeral lay at the end of the long, strange trip. I knew the Valley of Achor equaled a brand of death. And since I had dealt (in some small

138

portion) with the sadness of my mother's death in my desert, I was reluctant to go to another homegoing service. But I sensed God's internal, unrelenting prod. *Let's go all the way. Let's go to the bottom of the quarry. Let's go down to the valley. I'm here. Your valley of trouble can become a door of hope.*

It took me a long time—days and weeks and weeks and days—to finally get to the place of surrender, to the place of letting go. The "let it go" was at least partially experienced as "let *them* go," because as it turns out, I had unsanctified expectations of God *and* other people. And though I've never heard God speak audibly, it was as if he were writing on the walls of my heart, words like:

> Let them go. Let my people go from your heart. You are enslaved to them there. You have demanded too much of them. You have bent your life to them long enough. Daughter, though it may seem hard to believe, you have made idols out of good people, God people, but people nonetheless, people who were never, ever made to occupy that high place in your heart. Like the righteous rulers of old, destroy the high places. Bring them down, daughter. Topple them. Though you think letting them go will kill you, it will not. You will actually find life at this funeral. A door of hope is opening.

So I packed and followed God down deep into a desert valley. To my idols' funeral.

There I confessed that I had other gods in the form of others. Other people's opinions. Other people's affection. Other people's lives. Other people. I confessed it all. I had placed other people higher in my heart than I had placed the Most High.

139

This was a death, and like any death, I went through certain prescribed movements.

I memorialized what had been that I might count the cost— not of saying good-bye forever but of saying good-bye to imbalance, codependence, and overinvestment. *This is a hard good-bye but a needful one. So much has been so beautiful. I thank you for what has been healthy, and I ask you to reset the bones that are broken.*

I experienced dust to dust. I committed them back to God, some days gently, some days violently, as I tossed numerous people into the cupped hand of grace, the only ultimate safe place. *They are yours. They have always been yours. They were never mine in the first place. Take them back from me.*

I counted the cost of letting go and moving forward. *Things will be different now. Space will come. And it may bring a sting with it. The first flushes of absence. Apartness. Some necessary distance. And it'll feel like an echo of death each day, but that is as a funeral should be. Death will ultimately give way to new life. Like resurrection. A new normal.*

I threw in my rose before the last shovel of sand covered the relational idolatry. In the Valley of Achor, I buried my heart's idols. In the desert, I said good-bye.

And then I began the long, quiet journey out.

And after the wild wind of grief had blasted through my heart and blown me sideways, I sat on my desert couch a bit differently. Emptied out and yet expectant for the infilling. Raw and exposed. Like a newborn. Newborn heart. Newborn skin. Newborn eyes.

I believe that this new and surprising freedom from relational idolatry was preeminent above all the other benefits of my desert experience. I had been heartsick with many lesser things, but idolatry had been the big wound, whereby intimacy with

Jesus had been leaking away drop by precious drop. I had made other people the mediators between me and him, and now I had one mediator again. "For there is one God and one mediator between God and mankind, the man Christ Jesus" (1 Tim. 2:5). I could begin the journey back to intimacy.

Intimacy Restored

One fine day I read these category-busting words from the Christ: "I no longer call you servants, because a servant does not know his master's business. Instead, I have called you friends, for everything that I learned from my Father I have made known to you" (John 15:15).

The word translated "friend" is from the Greek word *philos*. *Strong's*, a study concordance, paints a beautiful picture of the interior roominess of the word Jesus uses. That simple word *friend* means a great deal said in Jesus's voice. *Philos*—"a friend; someone dearly loved (prized) in a personal, intimate way; a trusted confidant, held dear in a close bond of personal affection."[9]

I remember when it sank into my sinews that, relationally, Jesus was my friend and, more radically to my little mind, that I was his. I was Jesus's friend. He said so in John 15.

For years, I had engaged in a tricky dance with the close relational proximity of friendship. Friendship, as a concept, had always been a smidge baffling to me. I moved a bit growing up and had some serious run-ins with "mean," which caused friendship as a concept to be dangerous and untrustworthy. So on the one hand, I gave friendship (and sometimes people in general) the stiff-arm. On the flip side, when I was older and sent down roots, I tended to connect with friends too deeply and quickly.

For much of my life, friendship developed around a shared goal, which for me happened to be the intense experience of mounting theater shows. As a very intelligent counselor just pointed out to me recently, the intimate friendships fostered in these kinds of scenarios are by necessity fast, and, he continued, fast intimacy can crumble as quickly as it is built. Fast intimacy was the order of the day for much of my life. My friendship pace was set on F-A-S-T. So friendships (again, I speak generally; I also have lifelong friends whom I treasure) tended to be touch and go. Intense and quick. And then there were those other times when I turned friendship into an idol. So calling friendship tricky territory for me is like saying I am a tall, pale, nearing-menopause mom. One quick look confirms that.

Perhaps that is one of the reasons why I'd been able to see myself in other easily definable roles in terms of relatedness to God: a servant, soldier, learner, warrior, child, daughter. But friend? Friend? Really? An intimate confidant of almighty God?

I don't know that it is possible to overstate the paradigm-shifting power of Jesus's words in John 15. God, wrapped in human flesh, is . . . my friend? I can actually know his secrets? Be privy to his business? Surely, this must have been as upending a revelation as when Jesus taught his disciples to call Yahweh, the One who dwells in unapproachable light, Father, in what is commonly called the Lord's Prayer.

So God is my Father. Jesus is my friend. And the Holy Spirit is my paraclete, my helper. Father. Friend. Helper.

I fear, too often, that we take these appellations for granted. We dumb down their revelatory nature, casually thinking, *Jesus is my bro. And God is my sugar daddy in the sky. The Spirit is my wingman.* We make such intimacy reductive, easy to hold in our human hands. If we can grasp it in our hands, then we can

142

intellectually grasp it, right? But, truth be told, such intimacy is hard to fathom. The Almighty desires intimacy with me? He wants me to come in close? We cannot hold such revelations in our human hands; we can only come face-to-face with them. To understand them, we must experience them. Like Moses. Like the woman at the well. Like the nation of Israel in Hosea, who also received a revelation of intimacy. An invitation too.

"In that day," declares the Lord, "you will call me 'my husband'; you will no longer call me 'my master.'" (Hos. 2:16)

God offered his people the same beautiful invitation to a deeper, more intimate relationship. And he compared it to the most intimate relationship there is—that of a husband and a wife. God would be a husband who pursues, like Hosea. A husband who ransoms an enslaved woman, like Hosea. A husband who stays faithful when his wife is anything but, like Hosea. Here not only do we see the foreshadowing of Jesus as the Bridegroom and the body of Christ as the bride but we also see the heart of God, a heart that burns for restored intimacy with his people.

God was bringing the people of God, made in the image of God, back to the heart of God, which is where they had always belonged.

He was also telling his people, "Before this moment, you knew me in a certain way. You knew me as master, overlord, and now there is something more." The term *master* has an interesting backstory, and its meaning is not as obvious as it might seem at first glance. When I first read this verse, I thought Ruler, King, Almighty God, which God certainly is, but here the Hebrew uses a very specific word. You'll probably recognize it. *Master* literally means "after baal" or "Baal." This is astounding. God was saying, "My people, you have known me as a master, a baal, a false God. Your relationship with me has been tainted by your relationship with an idol. You thought I was just a big baal. You thought I was just an idol. Fickle. Demanding. Cruel. Withholding. Perhaps perverse." Then he gave them a new, surprising term of endearment for them to call him: Husband. One who woos. One who covers. One who rescues. One who weds.

We can experience the same movement in the desert—from idolatry to intimacy, from master (Baal) to husband.

Want the reorienting experience of true intimacy? Be willing to go to any desert Jesus invites you to, and to walk down into the Valley of Achor.

Attend a desert funeral that will bring you back to life.

Reflections

A brother questioned Abba Poemen in this way, "My thoughts trouble me, making me put my sins aside, and concern myself with my brother's faults." The old man told him the following story about Abba Dioscorus, "In his cell (cave/dwelling) he wept over himself, while his disciple was sitting in another cell. When the latter came to see the old man he asked him, 'Father, why are you weeping?' 'I am weeping over my sins,' the old man answered him. Then his disciple replied, 'You do not have any sins, Father.' The old man replied, 'Truly, my child, were I allowed to see my sins, three or four men would not be enough to weep for them.'"[10]

On the surface, this is a short story about taking the log out of your own eye that you might help your brother remove the speck from his. In other words, don't concern yourself too much with others. Look to yourself. That was certainly a part of my desert journey: "Take your eyes off your idols and look to yourself. And then look to me." Also interesting in the story is the copious amount of grief spilled out over one's sins in repentance. This reminds me so much of the Valley of Achor and the tears of a holy funeral.

Has the Lord shown you any idols that might be lurking in your life? Have you ever gone down into the Valley of Achor and allowed God to take them from you? Explain. How do you feel about intimacy with the Almighty? Do you feel it is available to you? Why or why not?

9

Solitude

The man who flees and lives in solitude is like a bunch
of grapes ripened by the sun.

Moses, desert father[1]

Jesus often withdrew to lonely places and prayed.

Luke 5:16

Silent Angels

I (almost) abhor silence.

I say "almost" because I am growing in this necessary grace
bit by bit. However, for most of my life, I have detested silence,
aka "the silent angel." I don't know when I first heard that
funny phrase—the silent angel—but it captured something I

had felt and feared for years. Perhaps you have heard of her—this so-called silent angel—if not encountered her firsthand. Likely, she has flown over you a time or two. She appears at the most inopportune times, like when you head out for what you know will be a fantastic dinner outing with a new friend only to realize that there is not a strong relational connection and that the conversational weight is squarely on your shoulders. If you don't keep the conversational motor humming, if you don't keep asking questions, the silent angel will descend. Silence will fall, and everyone will think, *This is . . . awkward. This is . . . beyond awkward.* With nothing to talk about, connection wanes, and the entire episode feels squirmy and uncomfortable.

So for years, I carried what I called "silent angel questions" in my purse. Kid. You. Not. I would announce that the silent angel could not be allowed to visit, and so I would offer some questions to stave off her appearance. Actually, after I pulled out the cards with questions on them (yes, real cards), often we had a lot of fun. What was your first concert? was always a favorite. It offered an innocuous and interesting sneak peek into what kind of world the person grew up in during their childhood. I've encountered an Elvis, Beatles, and the Beach Boys answer, which is pretty spectacular. Best teacher ever and why? (Quite often, believing in a student had more impact than a teacher's acumen in their particular subject.) On the whole, the silent angel questions were fun and harmless—good for a laugh and a little insight—but that doesn't mean I wasn't hiding a real aversion, which was an aversion to quiet.

And the desert is nothing if not quiet. Even in my particular desert, I could distract myself with visits and phone calls to a certain degree, and there was that one weird channel that played forgettable television shows from the early eighties, but after that . . . there was a lot of hushed quiet time. And quiet was just not something I was well acquainted with.

In my sojourn through the desert sayings, I was struck by how many of them revolved around silence. I encountered too many to do a fair sampling here, but the truisms ranged from the philosophical—"A man may seem to be silent, but if in his heart he is condemning others, he is babbling ceaselessly. But there may be another who talks from day to night and yet is truly silent, that is, he says nothing that is not profitable"[2]—to the pithy. I grinned when I read that desert father Agathon reportedly "for three years . . . lived with a stone in his mouth, until he had learned to keep silence."[3]

My desert experience didn't include chomping on a mouth full of rocks to keep me quiet. I had good ol' loneliness to accomplish that. In other words, since there weren't many people to talk to, I learned to be more physically quiet than I ever had been in my entire life. Like a desert father, sans the mouth stones, I was being trained in a necessary discipline—I was learning to keep quiet. And this quiet miracle would drive deep that second tent peg: restoration of the heart.

Five-Minute Challenge

> The LORD is in his holy temple;
> let all the earth be silent before him. (Hab. 2:20)

Just this Sunday, a pastor and counselor at our church, Jimmy Harris, taught on patience, and he spent a few minutes expounding on silence's place in developing patience, a necessary virtue in a world that does everything to knock one off one's patience game. Jimmy said he will often challenge

149

people to five minutes of quiet. No music. No phone. No distraction. No prayer. No mental checklists. Just quiet. For just five minutes. And, he added, he warns people to buckle up. We have such little space for silence that it is often surprising, sometimes shocking, what surfaces when given a chance. He also encouraged that, when practicing quiet, eventually, after some time, the silent angel will actually become a desired guest. Quiet begets more desire for quiet. And a quiet heart has room for Christ.

I had a lot of practice with quiet time on that desert couch, learning to lean into the mysteries of quiet and solitude.

Deeper In, Farther On

At first, all the quiet time I was experiencing seemed to magnify the emotional experience common to almost every desert I have read about or studied: loneliness. Deserts can feel incredibly lonely. Elijah dismissed his servant before he bounded into the desert, journeying into the wasteland without another soul. Jesus took no one with him into the desert as he went to face the enemy of his soul. It is likely that Moses was alone when he encountered the flaming foliage.

As I sat down with their stories, I wondered about these saints and the Savior and their obvious lack of companionship in their respective deserts. I began to wonder if they had tasted something I was just catching a whiff of. Maybe they understood that the desert is a journey beyond mere loneliness into something deeply precious—something that must be cultivated to be sustained spiritually—something like solitude. I wondered if by following these old and new covenant examples, perhaps I could discover—instead of a dry well of loneliness—an oasis of solitude. Perhaps I could exchange one for the other. To do that, first I had to examine the way I personally experienced both loneliness and solitude.

In my little world, the difference between loneliness and solitude can be summed up in the way I experience them emotionally. When I am lonely, my thoughts are largely consumed with people and places and a certain empty insufficiency. Something, someone feels absent. There is a palpable ache at the heart of my loneliness. Sometime in the 1800s, lonely came to include this verbal color: "dejected for want of company."[4]

Solitude, while certainly involving a sense of loneliness as well, actually comes from the word *solitudinem*, which can mean—wait for it—the desert or wilderness.[5] Solitude, it seems, is innately linked with the desert and the desert experience.

For me, I'm coming to see that while loneliness revolves around the absence of people, solitude revolves around the presence of God.

A Quiet, Slow Miracle

I wonder if Moses ever struggled with this tension between loneliness and solitude. And if he did, I wonder how long it took him to move from the driving ache from a lack of company to the realization of the blessed necessity of desert solitude with God. Was it at year ten in his forty-year desert sabbatical? Year twenty? Did Moses settle into solitude softly? Or did he battle its quiet ministry? What made the roar of the crowds and court fade in his ears? Did God use the consistent rhythms of a quiet shepherd's daily life—walking to find green pasture, standing beside the grazing flock, scanning the

151

horizon for predators—as a tool, day by day blanketing the noise that so often competes with God's voice? I'd wager that it took eons for Moses to embrace the power of a life rounded by solitude after such a noisy life as a prince of Egypt.

Solitude is best learned slowly. Daily. With empty space carved out for solitude's in-filling ministry. I don't know how long it took for Moses to learn such a life; I only see evidence that he did. He had an ear open to receive the voice of God when God spoke. And he must've learned a most important thing in his solitude about the voice of God: God speaks far more often in the midst of solitude than in the middle of the multitude.

Case in point:

> Now Moses was shepherding the flock of his father-in-law Jethro, the priest of Midian, and he led the flock to the far side of the desert and came to the mountain of God, to Horeb. The angel of the LORD appeared to him in a flame of fire from within a bush. He looked—and the bush was ablaze with fire, but it was not being consumed! So Moses thought, "I will turn aside to see this amazing sight. Why does the bush not burn up?" When the LORD saw that he had turned aside to look, God called to him from within the bush and said, "Moses, Moses!" And Moses said, "Here I am." God said, "Do not approach any closer! Take your sandals off your feet, for the place where you are standing is holy ground." He added, "I am the God of your father, the God of Abraham, the God of Isaac, and the God of Jacob." Then Moses hid his face, because he was afraid to look at God. (Exod. 3:1–6 NET)

The importance of this strange, fiery tête- à-tête cannot be overstated. Here the angel of the Lord converses with a man who forty years earlier had fled, a wanted criminal, from his place as an Egyptian prince and ruler and now lives as a mere "hireling shepherd, tending the flock of another man."[6] And yet God says, "Moses, you are the one. I choose you." God then proceeds to unveil his plans to act on behalf of his people, who have been crying out to him day and night in bondage. Because of this encounter, the Jewish nation remains to this very day, and you and I can claim a Jewish Jesus for our salvation and abundant life. The great exodus physically and the great exodus spiritually happened, at least in part, because God spoke in the desert solitude. And Moses listened, an ear trained by quiet.

Deep Desert

Years back, a pastor friend of mine directed my attention to a phrase in the first sentence of the burning bush encounter that deserves a closer look:

The far side of the desert.

Most likely, this was the writer's way of placing the encounter geographically—he was letting us know that this once-in-a-lifetime encounter happened far away, near the mountain of God. (Where this same humble shepherd would receive the Ten Commandments years on.) According to scholars, the text literally says that Moses was going "Horeb-way."[7] Perhaps Moses was taking his flock to graze in a place where they normally did not graze in an effort to be near the sacred mountain.

Something about that phrase—"the far side of the desert"—grabbed me like a five-year-old's surprise bear hug. In the original language, the "far side" literally means "behind or beyond the desert."[8] Some of us, in our desert experience, find ourselves going beyond the desert. It seems to stretch on a day (or a month or a year) longer than we think we can bear. We may wonder, *How long, O Lord, how far, O Lord?* but we keep stepping. Like Elijah, we travel forty days and forty nights in. We run the marathon. We hike the Appalachian Trail (sans the green trees and mountain streams) through the experience. We catch our breath, change our boots, slake our thirst, and get back at it. We covenant that whatever it takes—no matter how many days of solitude we weather—we will take the long way round, all in hopes of catching one whisper of him.

Taking the Long Way Home

A few months back, I was walking in my neighborhood. Even though I was talking to Jesus as I walked (something I desperately needed), I suddenly felt tired and thought the sky looked vaguely threatening, so I turned off from my normal course and took an unfamiliar path. I wanted the quickest way home. But as life would have it, the path meandered in a most nonefficient way, making my choice of a "shortcut" more like a "longcut."

As I continued winding through trees and serpentine paths, I became more anxious, and not a little bit frustrated, realizing I was going to be later—perhaps much later—getting home than I wanted. In that moment, I heard a familiar internal whisper: *I remember when you wanted to take the long way home.*

Even though I was tempted to start humming a certain 1980s pop song, I knew better. I knew that God was pressing something into the stuff of my heart, something that sounded like, *Allison, I remember when you used to stretch out our time together like taffy. I remember when you purposely communicated lavishly as*

*if you had all the time in the world. It's been more than a while since
you've wanted to take the long way home with me.*

Ouch.

Ouch, and yes.

I remember those first dates with my husband, Jonathan—
how when it was time to drive home, I secretly hoped he would
take the long way home just to stretch the moments of conversation and connection. What we talked about I can't recall,
and it doesn't matter. It certainly wasn't the heart of the thing.

The heart of the thing was that we just didn't want to leave
each other's presence—not just yet. We wanted just one more
song to wonder over. One more conversation. Just a few more
meandering turns before arriving at home. We wanted to take
the long way home because the long way home would give
us more of each other. More space and solitude to allow the
contents of our hearts to rise. To be spoken out. To be heard.

Jesus was saying all that to my heart and more.

He was saying, "Point-A-to-B living may be efficient and con-
trollable, but it isn't real life. *Real life* and *real relationship* take
time. Loads of it. And that doesn't change, no matter how long
you've been walking by my side. Let's get off the beaten path,
you and me. Let's take the long way home."

In other words, let's trek to the far side of the desert.

Space for the Speaking

This distant journey—this long walk of the Spirit, if you will—is
echoed in several of the powerful desert narratives we have
peered into previously. Elijah would have died spiritually without
the voice of God. He needed it like he needed the next moment
of shade and the water to quench the thirst that gutted him. He

was heartsick. Depressed. Questioning. On the verge of throwing in the towel. He needed some God wisdom and instruction. He needed the voice of God like the arid ground needs dew.

And the voice that changed everything did come—not on day one but forty days into Elijah's journey. After a long, deeply arduous and solitary journey, Elijah finally heard God—not in shuddering storms but in hushed overtones.

I have always been intrigued that God did not speak (that we see in Scripture) to Elijah in the aftermath of the showdown with the prophets of Baal, nor did he speak to him in the first day of the emotional and spiritual aftermath, when Elijah could barely turn his head for soup. True sound came as the noise siphoned from his heart like desert sand. A long walk to the far side of the desert made space in his heart for him to hear the voice that finally broke the long, dark silence.

Like Elijah, Moses also traveled to the far side of the desert, and it was on the far side of the desert that God revealed himself in the unconsumed bush. An average, normal thing—a bush—became an unconsumed miracle. And in that miracle was the very speech of the Sovereign.

How often have I been desperate to hear the voice of God but unwilling to journey very far to receive it? How quickly do I allow the noise to compete with what I most thirst for—an encounter with the voice of the Lord.

> The voice of the Lord shakes the desert;
> the Lord shakes the Desert of Kadesh. (Ps. 29:8)

When you're in your own desert, do you ever wonder what God might say?

God, I've found, will say whatever he wants. I've learned well that he will say what he will say. He is God, the uncreated One, who speaks and dark and light separate. We may go into the desert desperate to hear him speak on one subject, and he, in his sovereignty, will speak on another. We cannot control the voice of the Almighty; we can only position ourselves to receive it. And his voice changes everything.

Let me see if I can explain.

Euonymus Bushes and the Voice of God

As I've said previously, I've never heard the audible voice of God.

But I have heard him speak. And by speak, I mean communicate. Sometimes he uses the expected things—sermons, his people, prayer, and of course his written communiqué to us, the Bible. Most often, I would say I have felt communicated with through Scripture. But sometimes God plucks the strings of my heart through music or nature. After all, one of the longest books in the Bible is a book of song lyrics. And as for nature, well, Paul tells us that the very heavens communicate the presence and glory of God, so much so that we are without excuse if we do not acknowledge his existence (Rom. 1:20). I often think of the Magi who were told to follow an Eastern star, and Moses, who received a missive from the middle of a burning bush. God speaks one way and then another (Job 33:14). God will use anything to speak to us when he decides to speak to us.

About six years or so into my marriage, I went through a season of yearning—in all kinds of areas. Jonathan and I had left our Carolina home and had planted roots in Nashville— and we were doing all kinds of lifey, normal things. We sang a bit as a duo here and there. Jonathan was leading worship at our growing church. I was teaching acting students at a small college and a university in Nashville. In other words, things were happening and moving, but deep inside I felt deeply stuck.

It seemed like little in our lives ever "came all the way through." There were some false starts. There were bucket-loads of "almosts" and "nearlys." A ton of potential but not a lot of fulfillment. Pregnancies but no births. A lot of buds on the vine but no blackberries that I could hold in my hand. I need to emphasize that this was an internal struggle. To anyone else, my life would have seemed full and fulfilling. But internally, there was this ever-present desert ache. A pervasive dry patch. On the whole, life seemed like an airplane stuck in a holding pattern. And I didn't know what to do about it. The desert dryness we've talked about in earlier chapters existed in one area: the area of fulfillment. Of birth. Of spiritual victory. Of crossing the finish line.

I remember ruminating about this feeling to God. It had wriggled up through the ground of my heart's topography, in the solitude, and it stayed there exposed and sunburned. For. A. Very. Long. Time.

During this dry spiritual season, my grandmother's rural Carolinian proclivities came popping out of my hands and heart with a genetic vengeance. I was suddenly obsessed with all things seed and soil. If I bought one gardening book, I bought twenty. An inveterate learner, I soaked up information about what plants would weather our notorious Southern summers. I learned which herbs would be invasive. (No mint, ever.) I hired a young man to dig a giant bed in our front yard and tried to grow my own version of an English garden. I learned about soil amendment. Acidity and alkalinity. I learned about morning sun versus afternoon sun. About watering levels and pruning. (Oddly, pruning and deadheading were my favorites.) On and on it went. I, like a modern-day Eve, saw God in the garden.

At the back of my newly cut, front-yard garden bed were a couple of bushes that I had left as a bit of architecture. I loved the way the bushes held their own and created a vertical and horizontal backdrop for the wonder of my show-off black-eyed Susans and asters. At a certain point in the growing season, the leaves of my favorite bushes would turn green, then flame red, and then fall off for the winter. The bushes would remain stark and spindly until they would begin the process all over again.

I started noticing something odd about my favorite bushes one year, which happened to coincide with the year of the desert ache about fulfillment. In late fall, the red leaves of my Euonymus alatus (the bush's proper name) were not showing even the faintest hint of releasing. Odd. Red as flame, they were clutching the branches as if in a first-love embrace, even though fall had fallen. I thought this was unusual, especially since everything else in my garden was bowing to fall, dropping petals, browning up, hoarding for winter. I recall watching the bushes for a few weeks and determining with all my green thumbness that something about their positioning or the amount of sun they were (or were not) receiving was causing such leafy obstinacy. They refused to change seasons.

For weeks, I watched the bright red leaves' stubbornness, watching for any sign of release. There was none. My curiosity piqued, I began to be on the lookout for the same bushes all over Tennessee. (They were a popular landscaping choice.) Every bush that I saw had already dropped its leaves. I checked to see if some of them were in the shade like mine were. Many were. If they were up against buildings like mine were. Many were. In other words, in whatever soil or sun state I found the euonymus bushes, they had already given up their leaves. Everywhere but at our house. I commented on this horticultural oddity to Jonathan and shrugged my shoulders, proverbially. Weird, I thought.

One day, pulling into our little gravel driveway, I looked at the bushes—still bright red in the now-super-cool temperatures of fall—and thought, *That's just weird. That's beyond weird.*

And then I heard it—the internal voice of God, which in the few times I have heard it is louder than mere sound—as if he had scrawled words across the air. The voice pulled me up short behind the steering wheel as I sat looking at the bright-red bushes. *Child, your seasons are later than other people's seasons.*

Oh, friend, if I could tell you the number of times those words have lifted and sheltered me, I would. If I could tell you the profundity contained in those words that unfolded over the years, I would. In the thirstiest desert seasons, they were my water. They were my "*more.*"

You see, I wanted God to speak to the specific things I was worried about in that particular season. Specific plans I wanted to come through. Why I was watching others achieve their hearts' dreams, while I felt a tad overlooked. Why I didn't see more "obvious fruit" in my life. That's what I wanted God to answer—and he did, in his own way. ("Just hold on. It's not your time yet. Your seasons are much later.") But he also spoke something that would continue to unfold, like a piece of origami. Something so small that, unfolded, is actually something so large. This something that has been threaded through my life and has been as true as the sky's color is Truth that I carry—and that has carried me—to this day. "Your seasons are later than others."

My seasons have always been later than those of other people. My leaves hold on and drop late. I was a late bloomer physically and have always been one spiritually. I married later by evangelical Christian norms in the nineties (twenty-seven). I had babies later than most (thirty-three and forty-one). I started in Christian drama at thirty-nine and didn't feel called into a speaking ministry until forty-one. I had my first book published at forty-seven. I'll be near sixty when my littlest graduates from high school.

You see, when God spoke to me at around thirty-two, I knew none of what was to come. I hadn't even had my first baby. I just knew I wanted things to come to fruition in the same timing I saw in everyone else's life. But God was pressing into my heart, "Oh, my darling, they will. They will come to fruition. But things will happen in my way and in my time. And they will happen later than for almost anyone else around you. Your seasons are later. Don't push against that. Don't push against the later seasons. Embrace them. My miracles come quiet, and in your life, they will come slow. This is for your protection."

God spoke to me in my desert of solitude through the red-leaf bush called the Euonymus alatus.

Euonymus alatus, ironically, has a more common name: the burning bush.

Reflections

A brother asked Abba Sioses, "What am I to do?" He said to him: "What you need is a great deal of silence and humility. For it is written: 'Blessed are those who wait for him' (Isa. 30:18), for thus they are able to stand."[9]

The desert blessing of solitude has always been the most needful for me, and yet it seems to be the most difficult to carry into other seasons. Do you struggle to cultivate solitude? If so, how? What small thing might you shift to bring more solitude into your life? Do you believe that God seems to speak to his people more in solitude than in the middle of the multitude? Have you ever had the experience of taking the long way home with Jesus and journeying "beyond the desert"?

10

Recognition

Even if we are entirely despised in the eyes of men, let us rejoice that we are honored in the eyes of God.

Abba John, desert father[1]

The eyes of the LORD are on the righteous,
and his ears are attentive to their cry.

Psalm 34:15

Abba Ammonas was going to pay a visit to Abba Anthony one day, and lost his way. So sitting down he fell asleep for a little while. On waking, he prayed thus to God. "I beseech you, O Lord my God, do not let your creature perish." Then there appeared to him as it were a man's hand in the heavens, which showed him the way until he reached Abba Anthony's cave.

Ammonas, *The Sayings of the Desert Fathers*[2]

I remember the feeling as if it were yesterday. The excitement and the dread, all tangled up into one gnarly ball of adolescent feeling.

We agonized over dresses. Taffeta or faux silk? Tea length or knee length?

We agonized over hairstyles. Pinned up or let loose? Crimped or hot-rolled?

We agonized over heels. If you were a tall girl like me, especially heels. Flat? Modest pump? Sky-high heel?

To our thinking, any one of those choices could make all the difference between social acceptance and social exclusion. Particularly at junior high school dances. Most especially when the DJ announced the inaugural slow dance of the evening over the synth-bathed intro of an eighties song.

Your particular song may have been different, but I bet the moment was the same.

The lights would dim and the music would slow as the guys and the gals who were "going with" each other took the center stage under the sparkling disco ball. At the same moment, many of us would exit the dance floor, moving to the edge of the room—some standing, some sitting in the very same school chairs we would study *Romeo and Juliet* in come Monday morning. We waited as the fresh-faced guys looked up and down the line of chairs, taking us into account, figuring out who would (and who would not) be accompanying them onto the dance floor for the next three and a half minutes. We tried not to look too dispassionate or too desperate. Skittish wallflowers every one, we hoped our fashion and social choices would be perfect enough, just right enough, to bring about our deepest wish.

We were dying to be chosen.

Being chosen meant you had value. You belonged. Conversely, not being chosen brought insecurity, shame, and a few of its nasty friends. Being chosen was everything. Remember those days?

Looking back, I wonder if underneath the adolescent wish of being picked was a much deeper heart cry. *I wonder if we were really dying to be seen.* Could it be that underneath all the glitter and the effort, we were hoping and praying that someone would see us for us and choose us because of that?

And even now, as grown-ups, when we know better than to hang our hearts (and our value) on a three-minute slow dance, we still share something in common with our internal junior-high, wallflower selves, don't we? We are still dying to be seen. We are still hoping for someone to acknowledge us, to affirm us, and to say to us—no matter our age or the stage of our lives—"I choose you. You are not invisible. You are seen."

It seems that this particular need, this heart cry to be seen, was woven into our spiritual DNA from our genesis. Just ask Hagar. In the book of Genesis, we hear her harrowing tale.

Invisible Hagar

Hagar was a woman who had been cruelly mistreated and had absolutely no reason to trust the Hebrew God or his people.

> Now, Sarai, Abram's wife, had borne him no children. But she had an Egyptian slave named Hagar; so she said to Abram, "The LORD has kept me from having children. Go, sleep with my slave; perhaps I can build a family through her." (Gen. 16:1–2)

This is the first mention of Hagar in the Bible. And it's a particularly poignant introduction, knowing all that would unfold later. Hagar's story is still hard to read—even with thousands of years of biblical perspective and cultural understanding. But reading it can be nothing in comparison to what Hagar experienced living it.

Hagar was an Egyptian slave or maidservant, whom Abram likely "scooped up" while he was on an Egyptian stop. Abram was the patriarch of our faith, whom God had promised to make into a great nation. In fact, God had promised him that his offspring would be like the dust of the earth (and like the stars, uncountable and luminous). There was just one tricky problem with God's promise. Abram was childless, and his wife, Sarai, had had a dried-up womb for eons. Every passing year was another reminder of a promise deferred and unfulfilled. The couple was the walking epitome of the Scripture passage that says, "Hope deferred makes the heart sick" (Prov. 13:12). Sarai, Abe's wife, had succumbed to her heartsick state, and so after years of slow waiting, she took matters into her own wrinkled hands and came up with a quick fix, a solution that put Hagar, the Egyptian slave, in the hot spot of a spiritual desert sandstorm. Sarai's solution was bald: "Go, husband. Sleep with Hagar. Perhaps I can build a family through *her*."

The casual usage of another person for one's gain, though not uncommon at the time, still causes me to cringe. From the outset, Hagar was a commodity to be consumed, not a person to be considered. She was just a means to an end. Outrageously, Abram agreed. And did the deed. When Hagar popped her own positive pregnancy stick, the Bible says that Hagar began to despise her mistress, Sarai. You think? I wonder if Hagar knew that Sarai's intention—stated clearly to her husband—was to take Hagar's child as her own. Perhaps with each kick in the belly, Hagar thought, *You have forced me into "marriage," you have taken my freedom, and you will take my child. Despising you is the least of it, Sarai.*

Whatever the case may be, Sarai began to complain about the foul fruit of her own sinful actions to her hubby, saying, in effect, "Hagar is a teeny bit sideways in the way she speaks to me, plus *you*, Abram are responsible for this wrong I am suffering" (see Gen. 16:5). (Adam was a prototypical blame shifter, but his offspring, Sarai, was not far behind. First she blamed God for her barrenness; next she blamed Abram for Hagar's behavior. Wasn't the Hagar plan Sarai's brainchild? How unaware we can be regarding our own hearts.)

In this instance, Abram didn't have the wherewithal to stand up under Sarai's barrage, so he basically said, "Have at her. Have at Hagar. Do what you think is correct." And apparently, what Sarai thought was correct was mistreatment. The Bible records that Hagar fled into the desert, where the messenger of the Lord met her. Let's pick up the story there:

> The angel of the Lord met Hagar at a spring in the desert on the road to Shur and said, "Hagar, slave of Sarai, where have you come from and where are you going?"
>
> She answered, "I am running away from my mistress."
>
> He said, "Go back to her and be her slave." Then he said, "I will give you so many descendants that no one will be able to count them. You are going to have a son, and you will name him Ishmael, because the Lord has heard your cry of distress. But your son will live like a wild donkey; he will be against everyone, and everyone will be against him. He will live apart from all his relatives."
>
> Hagar asked herself, "Have I really seen God and lived to tell about it?" So she called the Lord, who had spoken to her,

"A God Who Sees." That is why people call the well between Kadesh and Bered "The Well of the Living One Who Sees Me." (Gen. 16:7–14 GNT)

Desert Recognition

Hagar had been emotionally battered and was bearing a baby for another woman. Abram, the progenitor of the babe, had given his wife carte blanche to mistreat her. The Bible doesn't specifically spell out the mistreatment, but the word that is translated "mistreated" is the ancient Hebrew word *anah*, and it means "to brow-beat" and "to depress."[3] The browbeating and depression of Hagar was so untenable that Hagar, with child, ran into the desert on the road to Shur, which, by the way, was the way back to her homeland—Egypt. If God hadn't "seen" Hagar, she probably would have died out there in the heat. Pregnant and alone. Without a friend in the world. No resources. No rights. No recognition.

Hagar was literally dying to be seen.

And then it happened—an angel of the Lord, which some scholars believe was an Old Testament appearance of Christ or even an embodiment of God himself, began to talk with her by a small spring in the desert.[4] It's kind of easy to blow past this moment and to move to what God said, but it is incredible *that* God said.

After God spoke to Hagar and gave her some hard-to-swallow instruction about going home—"Go back to her and be her slave"—as well as an audacious promise that the son she carried, though wild, would himself be a force to be reckoned with, Hagar cried out stunningly, "You are the God who sees me" (Gen. 16:13). This particular name of God, *El Roi*, is used only once in all of Scripture. Right here, in Hagar's story. A woman, a slave, a foreigner named almighty God. Hagar named God.

Our God sees the outsider. And the outsider sees God.

And the power of being seen doesn't stop with a revelation of God's character, as evidenced by the name *El Roi*. The Bible records that this occurrence was so momentous that the well nearby was named *Beer-lahai-roi*. It means The Well of the Living One Who Sees Me. The deep, deep desert cistern of water was named in honor of the One who sees, the One whose very being satisfies my thirst in the driest land.

Hagar could have named God many things after her desert encounter with him. God, my provision. God, my comforter. God, my wisdom. Surely, God is all those things and more. But rising to the top of Hagar's heart, the most important revelation of God's character in her dry and dangerous desert was this: he is the One who sees.

He is the One who recognizes me.

Holy Recognition

When I hear the word *recognition*, I always think of award ceremonies. Recognition, in our overarching use of the word, is almost always about crowning the winner, the wonderful, the winsome. Gold stars. Accolades. Medals. Tiaras. Ribbons. Statues. Plaques. On and on the modes of recognition go.

Achievement and success, I believe, are the dominant common language we speak as humans. There is nothing inherently wrong with that kind of recognition. The guy with perfect attendance or the girl snagging the world record for the 100-meter freestyle should most certainly be recognized for their incredible work. Merit deserves special mention. No doubt about it.

But the recognition I'm most interested in, and the type of recognition that, to me, is the most astonishing part of Hagar's story, is defined like so: acknowledgment of something's (or someone's) existence and validity, as well as identification of a person from previous encounters or knowledge.[5]

When God recognizes someone, it is not about merit; it is about intimacy and is done as a sovereign act of his will. I think of Jesus as he says to his followers, "You did not choose me, but I chose you" (John 15:16). I believe our intrinsic chosenness and recognition stem from one of God's first decrees, found in Genesis: "Let us make mankind in our image, in our likeness" (1:26). God's acknowledgment of our validity comes from his own decree and his own sovereign will. He recognizes us because we are from him, created in his image.

To that end, in Christ, we are stamped with the Maker's mark. Turn us inside out, and you will see the Imago Dei—the made-in-the-image-of-God stamp. If you were to take us to a spiritual *Antiques Roadshow* for authentication—for evidence of the Author or the Maker—they would find it. The appraisers, the authenticators, would flip believers over, look past the hairline cracks and the wear and tear, and find God's mark every time. And they would declare to everyone gathered around, "This one is authentic. I've found the Maker's mark. This is the real thing."

In addition, when God recognizes us, he knows us from previous encounters or knowledge. He knew us before we were "us" (Jer. 1:5). Our days were written in his book before one of them came to be (Ps. 139:16). He numbers every one of the overly processed hairs on our heads (Luke 12:7). He has future plans for us that are for good and peace (Jer. 29:11). We are known, recognized, validated in ways we can't fully understand. And that we may not fully grasp until eternity.

Hagar knew none of this before running away into the desert. Being recognized—or mattering—would have been the last thing on her mind as a runaway and mistreated slave. But being a nothing? Now, that I bet she was intimately acquainted with. I wonder about Sarai's browbeating, verbal blows. Do you? Useless? Stupid? Incapable? Whore? Usurper?

Then God found her, broken and bent, by a stream and recognized her—saw her for herself—and proclaimed a powerful verbal antidote to the repudiation she had long lived with: "Hagar, you will be the mother of a great nation. Call your son 'God hears.'" (Gen. 16:10–12, paraphrased).

You are seen. You are known. You are recognized.

Desert Delight

So what does the desert have to do with being seen, being recognized by God himself?

Everything. For me, often God has to take me to a barren place to strip me of counterfeit and false modes of mattering. Of performing. Of pursuing a place of preeminence in the world's economy. Somehow, I cannot seem to carry the gold stars and the pats on the back in the desert. They carry no weight there. And without those spiritual monkeys on my back, I can begin to reacquaint myself with the only recognition that matters—the Father's.

And, again, I sojourn into a desert symphony of silence, and the quiet consumes the false voices that compete with God's for supremacy in my life. Among its other benefits, the desert acts as a forced fast from false voices. God takes me to the silent desert because he is the only one who can fill me with true sound. The desert silences the noise that competes with God's voice.

I've been realizing lately how polluted I am. By noise. Noise pollution used to be the bane of city dwellers and airports, but now? The prevalence of and access to information and social media have made our world loud. We are exposed to so much more noise.

You post something that means something to you, and you get a certain number of likes (and a certain amount of released dopamine, a powerful neurotransmitter).[6] You feel alive! Validated! Recognized! Then you post something equally as important to you—perhaps a new venture—and nada. You feel crushed. One day your boss thinks you hung the moon. Tomorrow you are a total eclipse of the sun. For one event, you're the guest of honor. For another, you're left out in the wind. This is spiritual whiplash of the worst sort.

We are exposed to so many disparate voices and the reaction (or nonreaction) we garner from them. We know too much. There are too many voices in our ears, voices that often echo the unpredictable swings of the world and the unpredictable hearts of humankind. We are in a dark and dangerous echo chamber. And we wonder why we are so spun. So insecure. So shaky on our feet. So in need of an intervention, like Hagar. So confused, like Hagar. So in need of being recognized by a royal personage who does not bow to whim, who does not divide our lives into successes and failures, who does not change his love for us due to our performance.

We will never meet God and watch him fumble to remember our names or our stories. He doesn't have to work to recall us to his mind, because, as David reminds us, God's thoughts about us "outnumber the grains of sand" (Ps. 139:18). I've always assumed that David was speaking of the sand of a shore. And while that is certainly possible, it is equally possible that he was talking about the sand of the desolate desert.

Some of us need this realization of recognition so desperately, more than we need our next meal. We need to lose our ravenous hunger for human recognition and nestle into the truth of God's absolute recognition of us.

And to do that, we need to come in close. Perhaps closer than before.

Face-to-Face

When I was a young acting student at conservatory, one exercise caused a certain sustained level of discomfort. We would often be asked—very early in the morning, mind you—to choose a partner. Sometimes it was a partner with whom we had previously worked, and other times we were instructed to choose a new one. Whomever the partner, the exercise would commence. Sometimes we were asked to "mirror" each other. Whatever gesture or grimace the lead partner would make, the other partner would have to follow. The lead partner would try to move through their gestures slowly enough so that there was no difference between the leader and the follower. The endgame of the exercise was to jive as one person, as in sync as a reflection is with the person looking in the mirror. The "mirror game" I could hang with because although we were close in proximity, we were still focused on something else: we were focused on the movement and the matching.

173

But a few times we encountered a twist to the mirror game—one that made me as uncomfortable as a cat in a bubble bath! Sometimes our professors asked us just to look at each other. Knee-to-knee. Face-to-face. To take each other in. To note the shape of the eye, the arch of the eyebrow, the lift of the forehead, the angles of the hairline, the plane of the nose. One of the important skills for any actor is the skill of observation, and though this exercise was fairly rudimentary, it was a building block of learning to be observant. You can't learn to observe if you don't first look and see. So, duly, we looked and we saw.

The class in which we did this exercise most frequently happened far too early in the morning for any sane night owl. Most of us had barely rolled out of bed to slip in to class as the professor took roll. Hair was most likely askew. Sleep was often still residing in the eye. (Just keeping it real, people.) A white smudge of toothpaste often lingered at the corner of the mouth. All in all, this was a super vulnerable time to be doing a face-to-face exercise. We were definitely not camera—or even "mirror"—ready.

Looking back, I recall something peculiar: I had no problem taking in the foibles and physical particularities of whomever my partner happened to be. None whatsoever. I don't ever remember once thinking, *Gross,* or *They should try getting up a few minutes earlier,* or *Man, are those blackheads or freckles?* Nothing critical ever entered my mind that I recall. But when I felt like *my* foibles and faults and particularities and peculiarities were being taken in, oh, I wanted to run out of the room, abandon acting altogether, and consider a career as a dive instructor in Nova Scotia.

Turns out I had no problem seeing, but being seen was something altogether terrifying.

And yet in my own inhospitable desert, the *God who sees* was intent on this very thing. There was nowhere to hide on my desert couch. I had no choice but to sit cross-legged with God, knee-to-knee, face-to-face. And that turned out to be a very good thing in the end, because under his gaze, something started to shift. Something came out of hiding in me. He came in close, and I didn't run. I didn't turn my eyes away from his view of me. I didn't put on the spiritual sunglasses. I looked at Jesus, and, amazingly, I saw myself as he saw me, as someone much dearer, much more loved, much more significant, much more recognized than I had dared to dream.

Apples to Apples

In Scripture, an interesting phrase occurs multiple times depending on the translation. Maybe you've heard it. "The apple of the eye."

It's an archaic phrase that was used specifically in Shakespeare's *A Midsummer Night's Dream* as well as in different versions of the Bible. In our common speech, we would say that the "apple" is the treasured object. When Nana or a favorite aunt says, "You're the apple of my eye," she is saying, "You're my treasured thing." God said it of Israel: "He who touches you touches the apple of my eye" (Zech. 2:8 NHEB). David cried out, "Keep me as the apple of your eye" (Ps. 17:8).

It's such a wonderful phrase. And yet the meaning of being treasured above all others isn't the total tale. In olden days, the pupil of the eye was known as the apple, so the phrase "the apple of the eye" more accurately means "the center point of the pupil." Or the crosshairs of the view. So when God says that we are the apples of his eye, he is saying, "Child, you are in the center point of my sight. You are not on the periphery. Come gaze into the legitimate mirror that exists—my eyes and the way I reflect you back to yourself. Come see yourself there—in the apple of my eye."

Jonathan knew I was teaching on the apple of the eye and that I was desperate for a way for women to understand that, positionally, they are the apple of Jesus's eye and that if they would dare to come in close, they would discover this amazing truth for themselves. I was upstairs, and I heard a call from the tall man who had been editing pictures: "Alli, come here! You're not going to believe this." He had found something worth finding.

Do you see it? Both are absolutely unretouched. Do you see my older son, Levi, in the actual apple of Luke's eye? In the center point of his pupil? Would you take a second and soak

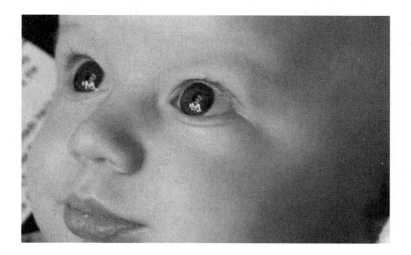

that in? See how at ease Levi looks? Saturated with brotherly love? Comfy in his own skin?

That is how God recognizes us. That, my friends, is how God sees us. You are always the apple of his eye and *in* the apple of his eye. Your beauty and worth are truly in the eye of the Beholder. The Beholder, of course, being God himself.

Holy Remembrance

Even after a quarter of a century of walking with Christ, I still stumble into situations when I wonder if he really sees, especially when I'm traipsing along the footpaths of an uncompromising desert, when I'm stranded in the veiled valley, away from his view. I think as long as our hearts are beating, we'll collide with moments like that.

But as I journey on, something is happening: my wallflower heart is giving way to a heart more like Hagar's. A heart that can exclaim, even in the driest, darkest circumstances, "There is a God who sees me." A heart that is restored by sitting down with this truth: if God sees me, then it truly doesn't matter who else does or doesn't.

And knowing that has made all the difference.

Oh, the unexpected gift of desert recognition.

Reflections

Always have God before your eyes.

Anthony, desert father[7]

Nothing in all creation is hidden from God's sight. Everything is uncovered and laid bare before the eyes of him to whom we must give account.

Hebrews 4:13

Reflect on a time you felt emotionally ragged and worn like Hagar. In that season, did you feel seen or invisible to God? In what ways do you feel recognized by God? Do you believe you have been stamped with the Maker's mark? How might you be a conduit of his grace for others going through a similarly difficult time? Do you believe your worth resides in the eye of the Beholder? Have you ever seen yourself as the apple of his eye?

11

Strength

It was related of Amma Sarah, that for thirteen years she
waged warfare. . . . She never prayed that the warfare
should cease but she said, "O God, give me strength."

Sarah, desert mother[1]

He gives strength to the weary
and increases the power of the weak.

Isaiah 40:29

From his entrance onto the national scene, hands full
of rocks, to the long years he spent running from a
maniacally enraged and jealous King Saul to his years
of military conquests, David was nothing if not God's athlete,
a phrase used by the desert fathers and mothers. When I think
of David, I see a life-size Stretch Armstrong man, carved and

muscled, who no matter how destructive the circumstances, bounces back. Spiritually and physically, David seemed to have an unbelievable amount of resilience and strength, even after some pretty billboard-sized failures. This strength extended to the moniker of his fighting men, the Mighty Men. Can you just imagine them—a super team of Olympic-level athletes, able to outrun and outfight just about any enemy? All of them were committed to a man who had not even sat upon the throne but who undeniably had the hand of God upon him. Listen to how one advisor described the king and his men to a usurping son: "You know your father and his men; they are fighters, and as fierce as a wild bear robbed of her cubs. . . . Your father is an experienced fighter" (2 Sam. 17:8).

Much of David's (as well as his mighty men's) training took place in desert locations. Under brutal circumstances. As they moved constantly. Scrounged for food. Strategized against an enemy with copious assets at his fingertips. An enemy who happened to be none other than King Saul. In this long desert season—thirteen years approximately—between the call and the crown, David and his men learned to fight by fighting stronger enemies who, by any rational odds, should have been able to whip them pretty handily. But fighting under impossibly trying circumstances, like ancient Navy Seals, David and his mighty men became skilled in war—fighters who could outlast and outmaneuver their enemies. The weapons that David possessed were honed and made effective in the desert—in times of suffering. David took all this hard-won, desert strength with him when he finally sat down on Israel's throne.

David was a man who was, in many ways, formed by the desert. And even after the crown and the expansion of David's warrior kingdom, he still found himself being trained by the rigors of the desert experience—physically and spiritually. Look at the song written by the man of strength during what must have been one of the most excruciating desert experiences of his entire life.

Psalm 63

A Psalm of David, when he was in the wilderness of Judah.

O God, you are my God; earnestly I seek you;
my soul thirsts for you;
my flesh faints for you,
as in a dry and weary land where there is no water.
So I have looked upon you in the sanctuary,
beholding your power and glory.
Because your steadfast love is better than life,
my lips will praise you.
So I will bless you as long as I live;
in your name I will lift up my hands.
My soul will be satisfied as with fat and rich food,
and my mouth will praise you with joyful lips,
when I remember you upon my bed,
and meditate on you in the watches of the night;
for you have been my help,
and in the shadow of your wings I will sing for joy.
My soul clings to you;
your right hand upholds me. (Ps. 63:1–8 ESV)

I can almost imagine the crackly voice of the king rasping out his soul's thirst for God's nearness, and I am particularly touched by the psalm's title: "A Psalm of David, when he was in the wilderness of Judah." It was as if David were saying, "I

181

penned this lament with my own hand. In the desert wilderness, I sang it with my own voice."

For a long time, I assumed that David's desert song was composed while he was being hunted by King Saul for thirteen years, but many scholars think Psalm 63 was likely written when David's son, Absalom, committed mutiny in the kingdom and was coming for his father's crown. They believe this partly because David refers to himself as king in the lyrics.[2] King David was in the middle of familial betrayal; the kingdom's tectonic plates were shifting as a beloved son, Absalom, made a run at the throne. The desert of betrayal was a desert of the highest and driest sort.

Into this particular Judean desert/wilderness, the people, as well as many fighters, followed the king (2 Sam. 15:16–18). These faithful Israelites understood the gravity of Absalom's uprising, and were joining in some form of communal support and grief as the kingdom crumbled.[3] Scripture renders the sad scene this way: "The whole countryside wept aloud as all the people passed by. The king also crossed the Kidron Valley, and all the people moved on toward the wilderness" (2 Sam. 15:23). At the end of his instruction to Zadok regarding the ark of the covenant, King David added, "I will wait at the fords in the wilderness until word comes from you to inform me" (2 Sam. 15:28).

It was perhaps during this desert night of the soul that David found himself seeking God again. Perhaps on this very night, as he waited for word about what to do, he composed Psalm 63. What a stunning road map for resilience and strength the aging king offered. In a desert of the soul, where betrayal had upended the order of life, David offered these simple principles in his desert song.

Seek

Though I am not proud of it, seeking God is often what disappears first when I am in a tough desert season. My first thing, my one thing, my Matthew 6:33 thing ("seek *first* his kingdom") moves quickly down the list of spiritual imperatives until it is bringing up the rear. My words—the expression of my heart to God, my prayers—seem to dry up like a drought-stricken Kidron brook. I misplace my ask-seek-knock. And yet here David said, "I will not only seek you but also seek you early." In those early watches of the night, perhaps when the betrayed king couldn't sleep, he was still making a priority of talking to the One who "will neither slumber nor sleep" (Ps. 121:4).

Friends, when you need a little desert strength, don't quit talking to God. Please don't. In your dark desert night, don't quit speaking out your heart to the only One who can do anything about the situation. "My heart says of you, 'Seek his face!' Your face, Lord, I will seek" (Ps. 27:8).

Remember

Laced throughout Psalm 63 is a theme of remembrance. David longed for the sanctuary, which perhaps he couldn't visit due to Absalom's rebellion. He remembered what it was like to sing with the Sons of Korah, "Better is one day in your courts" (Ps. 84:10). He also said that even on his bed, in the watches of the night, he would meditate on the One who had carried him through. He would remember.

One of the ways that I gained strength on my desert couch, or in times of desert grief, was remembering that God had been faithful. As a young woman, I kept a journal, and on occasion, I flipped through the pages to remind my soul that

God had been faithful and he had been good. I read scribbled prayers that had been answered—perhaps not always the way I had hoped but in ways I couldn't have ever imagined. I read journal entries of places I was stuck, and assumed I always would be, and discovered, by leafing through the anthology of grace, I was no longer mired. Even when nothing seems to bloom and the streams in the desert run dry, God does not run out or run dry, and he is ever and always working for my good. And for yours. Sometimes we just have to remind ourselves.

Worship

At almost every turn, King David reminded himself to worship. "I will sing for joy" is particularly poignant to me in light of his circumstances (Ps. 63:7 ESV). "My lips will praise you," "I will bless you," "in your name I will lift up my hands," "my soul clings to you" (vv. 3, 4, 5, 8 ESV). In the desert, worship may be the last thing we feel like doing and the thing we need the most. On my own couch, there were times I had to sing. I had to lift my hands. I had to worship my way through the desert.

Though very simple, seeking, remembering, and worshiping can bring streams of fresh water to our desert journeys, especially when we are in them being strengthened and being made strong in the meantime.

Contending as an Athlete

Syncletica, one of the desert mothers, said, "Those who are athletes must contend against stronger enemies."[4] Syncletica knew that to grow in strength, to become an athlete in Christ, an equal sparring partner would never do. Someone

184

far stronger was needed. Though we might not win, our abilities—acuity, strength, endurance, and so on—are being improved because we must reach beyond ourselves. When we train at our level, we will remain at our level. But when we train at a higher level—punching beyond our weight, lifting beyond our strength (safely and wisely, of course)— improvement follows.

When I was first learning to write, one of my mentors told me to workshop with the best around. In his sage opinion, a person never stretches as much as when they are writing with someone with a far greater command of . . . well, everything. Once, he even allowed me to workshop a first attempt at playwriting with his graduate students for one semester. Talk about a crash course in stretching and strength. (And humility!) I wasn't even living in the same country in regard to their ability and creativity, but merely being in their presence—hearing the way they imagined dialogue or constructed a dramatic arc—changed me for the better. A strength I did not know I had was nurtured and ultimately increased. And I grew in ways beyond someone merely believing in me (though this is powerfully good medicine). I grew because I heard something I aspired to achieve, and though the mountain was a steep climb, I took one more step than I thought possible. In a natural sense, I was experiencing what Isaiah wrote about: "He gives strength to the weary and increases the power of the weak" (Isa. 40:29).

Green or Purple?

I've got two sets of hand weights—purple and lime green—that have become particularly colorful bookends. They mock my embarrassingly weak arms, which have, over the years, been made weaker by a disc problem. After seven years of a half life physically, I finally had neurosurgery to replace the offending disc and the bits of disc that had lodged into the nerve canal. When I say I am at least part titanium, I kid not.

But back to the weights.

I had them for years, and on rare occasions, I would try to lift the three-pound weights. I would do so tentatively, always afraid that I might trigger a walloping, steroid-requiring spasm. Sometimes I could handle the three-pound weights, and other times I could feel the muscles revolting, threatening to knot up like the airport pretzels I long to scarf down at certain times of the month. So I would put the weights down. Light as they were, they were still too heavy for me.

And then I had surgery—successful surgery—and was cleared for all activity except, ya know, skydiving and moto-cross. After being so cleared, I lifted the three pounders with little ill effect, but there were still those purple five pounders. Taunting me. Testing me. And I thought, no way. There's just no way.

Until one day, for some reason, I thought there might be. The time had come to test what the doctors had told me. Carefully pumping the purple iron, I suffered no ill effects at all. Nothing that a little ibuprofen couldn't handle. I could lift more weight than I thought I could. I could handle more than I thought I could. I had more strength than I had possessed before.

One of the blessings the desert gifts us—one of the deepest means of restoration—is strength and confidence, a holy confidence that, in Christ, we are capable of more than we previously believed. We can confidently lift more "weight" than before. Some of us spend our spiritual lives lifting three-pound weights when Jesus is standing nearby whispering, "You are capable of more. In me, you are stronger than you think." He actually has more adventurous, albeit challenging, things for us to join him in, but he has to prove to us that we can bear the weight. In him. And sometimes to prove such a thing to our timid hearts, he walks us into the desert, where we have no choice but to go through the experience we are convinced we cannot weather, to "lift the weight," as it were. And when we do, we have the assurance that we can follow him into whatever comes next.

My damaged neck, in many ways, had been a physical desert for me: I had lost the joy of gardening, which had been a part of my life since I had first learned what it felt like to break open the earth. I had lost the ability to exercise, which, for a former performer, was difficult on an emotional level as well as on a purely physiological one. Staying physically fit was hard, as sometimes even a short walk could trigger a spasm. I was always afraid of missing a speaking event. I think you get the picture. It was a dry place, disorienting and unpredictable, as I'm certain the desert was for many of the biblical men and women with whom we have sojourned thus far.

But in that long desert season (along with other desert seasons), I found out two things: I know who I am, even when the things that previously defined me are stripped away, and, when I grab the hand of Jesus, I am stronger than I had dreamed.

Reflections

I pray that out of his glorious riches he may strengthen you with power through his Spirit in your inner being.

Ephesians 3:16

It is like those who wish to light a fire; at first they are choked by the smoke and cry, and by this means obtain what they seek (as it is said: "Our God is a consuming fire"): so we also must kindle the divine fire in ourselves through tears and hard work.

Amma Syncletica, desert mother[5]

Have you ever found yourself in a season of intense strength development? Have you ever been required, by Christ, to lift more weight than you once believed you could? How does a desert experience play into building strength? How might you find practical ways of worshiping, seeking, and remembering in your own desert night?

12

Beauty and Bounty

But as it is written:
> "Eye has not seen, nor ear heard,
> Nor have entered into the heart of man
> The things which God has prepared for those who
> love Him."

1 Corinthians 2:9 NKJV

So on the third day they planted a stick, and it sprouted
and bore fruit, and they all gave glory to God.

Cassian, desert father[1]

A s we begin to round our final curve, let's look at the
Scripture passage that we have returned to like a well-
worn travel guide: our desert walker's wellspring. This

time, however, I'd love for us to meander through these majestic words slowly. Languidly. Lovingly. Perhaps read them aloud so you can hear the "voice that shakes the desert" and be refreshed by the beauty and blessing you can discover in a sandy land.

> Therefore I am now going to allure her;
>   I will lead her into the desert
>   and speak tenderly to her.
> There I will give her back her vineyards,
>   and will make the Valley of Achor a doorway of hope.
> There she will sing as in the days of her youth,
>   as in the day she came up out of Egypt.
> "In that day," declares the LORD,
>   "you will call me 'my husband';
>   you will no longer call me 'my master.'
> I will remove the names of the Baals from her lips;
>   no longer will their names be invoked.
> In that day I will make a covenant for them,
>   with the beasts of the field and the birds of the air
>   and the creatures that move along the ground.
> Bow and sword and battle
>   I will abolish from the land,
>   so that all may lie down in safety.
> I will betroth you to me forever;
>   I will betroth you in righteousness and justice,
>   in love and compassion.
> I will betroth you in faithfulness,
>   and you will acknowledge the LORD." (Hos. 2:14–20
>   Oxford NIV)

Every desert season I have traversed with the Desert Walker has revealed incredible blessings—blessings in the going in, in the going through, and in the coming out. To recognize them fully is a slow dawning. These unexpected beauties unveil themselves degree by degree, but they are present nonetheless. I am learning to give revelation some time. For me, revelation comes slowly. I wonder if the same slow dawning happens when young soldiers exit boot camp. At first, they are just thrilled to be done with it, to allow the muscles and the psyche to heal from such strenuous use, to revel in the small freedoms they had been denied during such difficult training. But I also suspect that, at some critical point, when the training is *really* needed—like when they lock eyes with a real enemy—they give thanks for the blessing of such strenuous experiences.

In many ways, that's how I have felt about my desert seasons. At first, I am just happy to see rain and ground-breaking flowers, happy for the whole experience to be squarely in my rearview mirror. Certainly, I would not run right back to sign up for another desert go-round, but when I am faced with situations that need the rare gifts the desert has given me, I am so relieved that I can unwrap them when the right time comes.

Desert Oddity

During the writing of this book, as I hunted down the many appearances of the desert in God's holy narrative, I came upon a passage I know I must have read numerous times, yet somehow the words must've never dropped deep into me. Like discovering the desert fathers and mothers, noticing this particular Scripture passage was akin to discovering long-lost kin. Something in me leapt. Yet there it was—in all its confounding glory—at the end of God's instruction to Moses regarding the desert journey that awaited the people of God. Let's see what God declared:

> But I know that the king of Egypt will not let you go unless a mighty hand compels him. So I will stretch out my hand and strike the Egyptians with all the wonders that I will perform among them. After that, he will let you go.
>
> And I will make the Egyptians favorably disposed toward this people, so that when you leave you will not go empty-handed. Every woman is to ask her neighbor and any woman living in her house for articles of silver and gold and for clothing, which you will put on your sons and daughters. And so you will plunder the Egyptians. (Exod. 3:19–22)

Did you happen to notice who would ask the Egyptians for the plunder—the gold and silver and clothing, the very tangible blessings that would be put on their sons and daughters and carried into the desert? The women. The women were involved in the world's most gentle plunder ever, and the purpose of that plunder was so that the Israelites could carry blessings right into the desert of their freedom.

This odd instruction stuns me because it was given right there—while Moses was conversing with an angel in a burning bush in the far side of the desert. This wasn't some odd tactical detail tacked onto the end of a conversation as Moses approached Pharaoh with Aaron tagging alongside. No, this instruction was given during the details regarding the great exodus. Right up front. The Lord said, "Moses, you will be journeying into the desert to worship me, and the women will be the conduit for my provision and blessings, carried into the desert on the bodies of your sons and your daughters."

Blessings so oddly given—and so oddly gained.

The Once-and-Future Vineyard

We have looked in detail at how God uses the dry seasons in our lives to reveal and restore our hearts. Now, we need to speak of how he releases the heart. To unpack God's special brand of release, we need to peek into the specific blessings spoken of in Hosea—which are definitely on the intriguing if not altogether odd side. At least the first one is. Let's look at it.

> Therefore I am now going to allure her;
>   I will lead her into the wilderness
>   and speak tenderly to her.
> There I will give her back her vineyards. (Hos. 2:14–15)

This sounds fantastic, doesn't it? To be given something back. To be released into God's reciprocity? To have restored to you something that was always yours. Hosea says that Israel was going to be given back her vineyards. Right there, in the most arduous and arid experience a people group could ever endure, God made a promise of restored fruitfulness. And the promise was not diminutive. This was no puny garnish of a thinly sliced strawberry. Far from it. God was promising a vineyard—rows and rows of the good stuff. Acres of the sweetest grapes.

Vineyards are coming back to you in your desert, daughter, vineyards that should probably be growing anywhere but.

When I first began to investigate the desert vineyards that were promised, I mistakenly thought they were poetic hyperbole, a

193

way of metaphorically saying to the people of God, "You cannot imagine the amount of fruitfulness into which God can release you—even in the driest circumstances. It's so enormous that you will not be able to bear hug it. You cannot even dream it up. It's as if you will wake up one morning only to find rows and rows of perfectly green, hydrated vines bearing sun-sweetened grapes." That's what I thought about Hosea's particular vineyards. Holy exaggeration. Grand imagery. Because, let's face it, as far as we know, vineyards do not usually thrive in the desert. The Bordeaux and Rhone Valleys in France are not deserts. Tuscany is not a desert. The Napa Valley is not a desert but a fertile valley.

Vineyards do not grow in the desert. Except when they did. Which, apparently, they did.

The Bible is brimming with references to grapes, vineyards, and wine. The deserts, at least in part, were lined with vineyards. Recorded in the book of Numbers, as Moses sent people to check out the Promised Land, they brought back one cluster of grapes so large that two men had to carry the thing *on a pole*. Oddly, one of the Bible's most fatally prophetic events revolved around the illegal seizure of a vineyard. Ahab and his wife, Jezebel, plotted against an innocent man named Naboth to steal his vineyard, and, because of the theft, judgment was pronounced against the line of Ahab (1 Kings 21).

Writer Rebecca Fineman says, "Remnants of wine presses found in Israel dating back 8,000 to 10,000 years reflect the long history of winemaking in the region. By the time Rome grew to power in the 8th and 7th centuries BCE, Israel's wines had become noteworthy and were being exported to Rome."[2] Fineman goes on to point out that as Israel was occupied by foreign peoples, the art of making wine was largely lost—as were her vineyards.[3]

And now those vineyards are returning.

The entire wine industry is apparently making a comeback in Israel in, you guessed it, the middle of the desert. Dan Savery Raz writes in a BBC article, "Like most Middle Eastern deserts, the Negev is usually associated with sand, rock and the odd camel. However, this seemingly dry and arid region in southern Israel is now home to a burgeoning wine route, thanks to a group of pioneering 21st-century farmers and their use of computerized drip irrigation."[4] This unusual area is sometimes referred to as the Negev Desert Wine Route, or more commonly, the Negev Wine Route.[5]

I wish you could see pictures of all these verdant vineyards smack dab in the middle of the desert. Green swaths spread upon tan floors. Leafy life sprouting alongside apparent death. It is such an odd-looking mash-up: two things that should not coexist and yet do.

The desert, paradoxically, is breaking into fruit.

Vineyard Vitals

I am no viticulturist, and what I know about vineyards and grapes could half fill Thumbelina's thimble. When I hear experts speak of legs and acidity and grape combinations, my eyes glaze over. But in reading about vineyards for this book, I happened upon some interesting material written by Luiz regarding soil depth and drought stress that fairly screamed "desert vineyard." See if you concur.

> Soil depth . . . comes next. . . . Thus, such a soil must be 5 feet or more in depth, while sandy soils must be considerably deeper to supply enough water to the vine. How does it

affect the quality of a wine? There's been ample demonstration throughout wine regions of the world that a mild (but not excessive) water stress during the ripening period of the grapes is favorable to wine quality, and good viticultural practices can optimize the outcome. . . . Chile's Vigno Cooperative in the Maule Valley grows Carignan without irrigation and the roots of those vines have grown deep enough to allow the vines to survive the hot and dry Chilean summers without any major water stress. Not only that, the vines produce grapes of intense color, ripe phenolic compounds, and good concentration of aromatic and flavor pre-cursors, showing that a characteristic of the soil (in this case, depth) can improve the quality of a wine.[6]

Ripe phenolic compounds aside, the upshot of this excerpt is this: roots have to burrow deeper into sandy soil to reach the water source, and that root depth can cause a sweetening of the grape itself. In addition, one mild water stress event (i.e., lack of water) can also affect the favorability of the grape crop. Both of these "vineyard vitals" can happen in the desert, which is the very embodiment of the sandy soil spoken of here. Plus, there is certainly not a lot of rainfall and certainly a deeper root system.

No sour grapes here. Only fruit sweetened by the struggle.

Oh, and something else: desert fruit has a long shelf life. It lasts a really long time.

Forever Fruit

I cannot help but think of Jesus's beautiful statement at the Last Supper, made just prior to his breaking the bread and lifting the cup full of crushed, vineyard fruit: "You did not choose me, but I chose you and appointed you so that you might go and bear fruit—fruit that will last—and so that whatever you ask in my name the Father will give you" (John 15:16).

You and I have been chosen and appointed to bear fruit—and the fruit appears to be a long-living varietal, because, as Jesus says, it is "fruit that will last."

It is interesting to note that grapevines, by nature, are extremely long-living plants. Well-cared for, one grape vine can thrive, sometimes up to a hundred years.[7] In other words, they last. For generations. The astounding desert fruitfulness that God cultivates is about so much more than our lives and our concerns and our fill-in-the-blanks. That would be enough if God had deemed it so. One generation would be amazing. But this is a multigenerational God we know who often introduces himself as the God of Abraham, Isaac, and Jacob. No wonder, then, that under his watchful care and "green thumb," if you will, this fruitfulness, this restored desert vineyard, will bear fruit for generations. This is fruit for our kin and kindred. For our friends and families. This is forever fruit. What I have cultivated in the desert can be passed down to my children and their children.

Desert daughter, your desert is breaking into vineyards—rows and rows of fruitfulness. And that is not all. He also releases us back into first love.

Fluttery Heart

When I ran headlong back into the embrace of Christ as a young woman, I couldn't wait to run through the open doors of church. Some people look forward to Friday like an escape hatch for the week. Me, I jonesed for Sunday. The Son's Day. I would often wake wide-eyed in the dark, wee hours of a Sunday morning, disappointed that it wasn't time to get up yet.

> I rejoiced with those who said to me,
> "Let us go to the house of the LORD." (Ps. 122:1)

> Better is one day in your courts
> than a thousand elsewhere;
> I would rather be a doorkeeper in the house of my
> God. (Ps. 84:10)

> Awake, harp and lyre!
> I will awaken the dawn. (Ps. 108:2)

> O God, thou art my God; early will I seek thee. (Ps.
> 63:1 KJV)

I was about all of that. Give me one glad day with you, Lord, the earlier the better. If I can awaken the dawn itself, consider me the day's human alarm clock. I think you get the picture. My heart thumped with the vitality of first love.

Musical worship, particularly, was the air I breathed. I lived for it. In my church, we all seemed to. We lifted melodies— not to be heard by our neighbor but by Jesus himself. Off-key. Out of tempo. Whisper soft. Bullhorn loud. It mattered not a whit. It was not the perfection of the singing but the purpose of the singing that mattered above all. Singing was a mandate. A must.

Those songs were more than just mere songs. They were snatches of my heart lifted on holy tune, moments too expansive to merely speak, histories and hopes that needed to be released from the heart. And the song was the best releasing agent around. To this day, though it is still musical worship that pries open my heart and lifts my hands into the negative space of the air, there was something—something unique—about how I sang to Jesus when I was young. We've been told young love only comes once. It never comes again in quite the same way—or does it? Once taken from us, can our hearts ever beat with the same breathlessness? Can our young songs be restored to us? Hosea seems to say so.

> Then I will give her her vineyards from there, and the valley of Achor as a door of hope. And she will sing there as in the days of her youth, as in the day when she came up from the land of Egypt. (Hos. 2:15 NASB)

When the people of Israel came up out of Egypt, in a way, they came up singing—carrying the plunder of Egypt, going to worship God on the mountain of God. Then after the miracle of the Red Sea crossing, there was first Moses's song and then Miriam's song. They had been given a desert song.

Strange as it may seem on the surface, something about weathering the desert terrain with Jesus gave me back a youthful song as well. Let me see if I can explain. Most everything about the desert was emotionally trying, draining me of my song, but as I was being released by Jesus, I felt a melody sneaking its way up through the sand. The song sprang up from a wellspring of gratitude—gratitude that we (Jesus and me) had made it through, that Jesus had not only carried me but also covered me. When the desert heat was required to burn out some things in my life, he allowed it. When I needed a cave in which to gather my strength, he provided it. When I thought I would perish from lack, he provided manna. When I toted idols around unaware, he invited me into a valley funeral that would end in resurrected life. He said, "I recognize you," even when I didn't recognize myself. When my perspective was shoved into tight, worldly places, he nudged me back out into the open landscape of his perspective. He did such fruitful work in my desert that bursting into song seemed the only option.

I once had a teacher who taught us newbie theater kids a lesson I'll never forget. He wanted us to understand that when characters break into song in a musical, it is largely because they *have* to break into song. The moment is too large for mere speech. The largeness of the emotion causes a new level of expression. I've never forgotten the lesson, and I think it is oddly fitting for the release God provides in our deserts. For me, the desert experience was too big for speech. It required song.

We, too, have been through something that requires song. Perhaps something both more exacting and more excruciating than we have ever known before—the desert experience. Perhaps an experience we did not quite know if we could—or would—weather, and, miraculously, because of the enduring grace of Jesus, we have. Oh, have we. We've traveled through the long, hot season—something we would have bet our last pair of walking shoes would have broken and shaken us to the core. Stolen our song. Stolen our dance. Stolen our hope. But it did not. Miraculously, here we stand. Sunburned, perhaps. Son-soaked, certainly. We exit the desert different people. Changed. Bountiful. Empty-handed and miraculously loaded down with gifts.

Gratitude for all I experienced released me into song. I began to sing (or respond), as Hosea wrote, as in the days of my youth. And though I was forty-one and emerging from the desert of the couch, somehow I was a nineteen-year-old girl all over again, waking in the early hours, ready for the doors of God's house to be open. My knees creaked but my heart cranked out a tune. My song, so long silent, began to soar again.

I have been reading multiple articles recently that suggest that people who sing are somewhat healthier and happier than their nonsinging counterparts. Why that might be so is still being debated. Some researchers and writers posit that singing is largely a communal effort, and so, when we sing, we commune with people, and the positive benefits of community have been proven and proven again. Other researchers found that certain neurochemicals are activated when we sing.[8] There are even specific neurons that researchers are calling musical neurons that appear to respond specifically to music.[9] I always say that whatever we think we know or discover, God arrives first. In the English Standard Version of the Bible, the word *sing* is used 209 times. The book of Psalms, one of the lengthiest books of the canon, is essentially a lyric book. Our song, our singing, is critical to our health, and God says, in his outsized creative way, that I am going to release you back into song.

Trust that the desert is able to release you back into song. It's time to sing again, daughter.

Desert Blooms

For years, there was an odd-looking plant in our house in a simple terra-cotta pot. Its position shifted around a bit—top of a shelf, shadowy corner by the TV. The dark-green specimen grew in fleshy segments that were attached by thin filaments of plant material. It was, for sure, nothing fancy. A deeply forgettable plant. It blended into the background of books and figurines and other whatnots. Its soil was compacted— like dull, black concrete. It required only a drip-drop of water, whenever one might get around to it, and it seemed that no abuse dished out on the poor thing could cause its demise. When I would get into a rare cleaning frenzy, I would want to trash it. But Mom would protest, usually moving it back to a particular sun-drenched spot on the fridge.

And then it would happen. The thing would pop out flowers like little red umbrellas, one at each joint. My mom called it a Christmas rose (even though it's technically called a Christmas cactus), because around Christmas, it would bloom. At the advent of Jesus, the deadest-seeming things bloom.

Especially in the desert.

I happened upon an article—just yesterday—that snatched from me my proverbial breath. It echoed what the blooming cactus taught me but writ large. Strike that. Writ God-sized. I blinked twice when the picture scrolled across my screen; the discovery was as surprising as when I discovered that there were actual vineyards fruiting in Israel's desert.

A little backstory, if I may.

The Atacama Desert in Chile is so dry that in some spots in its particular geography no rain has ever been recorded. You read that right. Ever. Not so much as a drop of rain. This is a super desert. And, after a huge rain, this super desert, apparently, just broke into super bloom. I'll let writer Sarah Gibbens, in this *National Geographic* article, render the floral oddity in her own words:

> One of the driest regions on Earth has transformed nearly overnight from a sparse desert into a beautiful garden of many

colors. That's because heavy rains in mid-August have caused thousands of flowers to bloom.

This periodic phenomenon in Chile's Atacama Desert is known locally as desierto florido (flowering desert). . . .

Tourism officials told the BBC it's possible more flowers will bloom in coming weeks because some species germinate later than others. Over 200 different types of flowers can be found in the desert.

Super blooms aren't unique to Atacama. They occur in deserts that contain a large number of flowers called perennials (and sometimes called ephemerals). The blooms, while striking, are characteristically short lived, due to the harsh desert environment.

Seeds in desert perennials often lie dormant for months or years, alive, but unseen. It's only when rainwater washes the protective coating from their seeds that they begin to sprout. Earlier this spring, Chile saw torrential rainfall, creating the perfect conditions for a bloom not expected for several more years.[10]

Um. This small article is a master class in the hidden blessings of the desert. Two hundred varieties of flowers. Two hundred types of seeds that lie dormant. Sometimes lying dormant for years. Seeds that break into bloom at the first major desert rainfall.

Dear desert sojourner, I would love for you to imagine that the blessings of the desert—the shifted perspective, the strength, the solitude, the revelation, the recognition—can function as seeds in your life. Hidden in Christ, they are ever at the ready to burst forth into glorious life at the first sign of rain. Try to think of them as seeds in this regard too: seeds are portable. Seeds can travel with you out of the desert. You can drop them in your pocket and plant their self-contained gifts in other seasons. Seeds are transferable and can also be gifted to others. When your sister or brother journeys into their own dark night of the soul, you can pull them to the side and whisper, "I've been there. Here, take these with you. Experience them. Plant them. Wait on them. They will break into the most vivacious bloom when the rain comes again. And it will come again."

In Jesus, even the desert blooms.

Walking Out

Oddly, I don't remember the specific date I was set free from my three-month desert sojourn. I only know that sometime in October, after nearly three months of solitary and "Sovereign" confinement, I was released. The time had come to reenter the daily world. To prove the momentous occasion of social reentry, a friend snapped an over-the-top, tickled-pink picture of Jonathan and me at a harvest festival . . . in costume. In haste, I had decided that my costume would be a few freckles, two side pigtails, and a red shirt. I looked like the world's largest pregnant Daisy Mae—sans the inappropriate booty shorts and the attendant twang. Mostly, though, what I notice about the picture is that we look like two exhausted but thankful people, people who had walked out of the desert and could not believe they had made it.

It became clear that the cerclage—the procedure that had been done to hold the pregnancy structure—had done its job like a boss. Against the odds, it had held. At around thirty-seven weeks, the doctor took the cerclage out. Finally free, I was encouraged to walk a little bit and to resume normal activity (as much as a forty-one-year-old pregger mama rolling at 241 pounds could). And to wait for the coming due date.

Bed rest had done its job for my body and for Luke's. And the desert had done its job for my spiritual health. I came out loaded down with blessings, which I hope this book has, in part, unpacked for your heart—blessing upon desert blessing, the biggest of which I was about to give birth to.

On November 9, 2011—at thirty-nine weeks—we drove to the same hospital where my baby's life had been saved, and we checked ourselves in. I remember thinking, *I had no idea we were actually going to make it.* As the birthing process progressed, a grand irony ensued, as I had to be induced to get my body to go into birth. It seemed to surprise everyone in the delivery room that my baby was so stubbornly hanging on to life in the womb. After all, there was little to no cervix left. My babe wanted to stay.

Strangely, there were parts of me, too, that "wanted to stay," that looked back on the desert with fondness, longing even, odd as that may seem. I could not have foretold the DNA-level work of God there. I could not have imagined being laden down with such unexpected blessings that come no other way save through the desert.

The time for birth had come, and I pushed for all I was worth, with Jonathan coaching me with every breath. And as is the way of such things, a baby—a redheaded baby named Luke—came forth, releasing a wallop of a cry.

He was finally released. I was finally released. My heart was finally released.

> Lasting fruit had been born.
> Thirst had been satisfied.
> The desert, so hard, so beautiful, so full of unexpected
>   blessing.

Acknowledgments

Jonathan: My proof.

Levi and Luke: My joy.

My extended family. My dear friends. My church: My net.

Lisa Jackson, Vicki Crumpton, Wendy Wetzel, Kristin Kornoelje, Revell: My gratitude.

Emmanuel: My song.

Notes

A Desert Walker's Wellspring

1. Some versions have "comfortably," which will become important a bit later on.
2. Achor means "trouble." Oxford NIV Scofield Study Bible, ed. C. I. Scofield (Oxford: Oxford University Press, 1984), 893.
3. The word *sing* here can also mean "respond." Oxford NIV Scofield Study Bible, 893.

Chapter 1 Spiritual Deserts and Leather Couches

1. *The Sayings of the Desert Fathers*, trans. Benedicta Ward, SLG (Kalamazoo, MI: Cistercian Publications, 1984), 124.
2. Keith Beasley-Topliffe, ed., *Seeking a Purer Christian Life*, Upper Room Classics: The Desert Mothers and Fathers (Nashville: Upper Room Books, 2000), 6.
3. Ibid., 6–11.
4. Hebrew Dictionary (Lexicon-Concordance), accessed February 1, 2018, http://lexiconcordance.com/hebrew/6601.html.
5. *The Sayings of the Desert Fathers*, 125.
6. Ibid., 205.

Chapter 2 Desert Whats and Whys

1. www.goodreads.com/quotes/1099257-the-truth-does-not-change-according-to-our-ability-to.
2. *The Sayings of the Desert Fathers*, 42.
3. David Scott, "Mother Teresa's Long Dark Night," in *The Love That Made Mother Teresa* (Manchester, NH: Sophia Institute Press, 2013), https://www

.catholiceducation.org/en/faith-and-character/faith-and-character/mother
-teresas-long-dark-night.html.

4. David Van Biema, "Mother Teresa's Crisis of Faith," *Time*, August 23, 2007, http://time.com/4126238/mother-teresas-crisis-of-faith/.

5. *The Sayings of the Desert Fathers*, 249.

6. Ibid.

7. qbible.com/hebrew-old-testament/hosea/2.html.

8. Ibid.

9. *The Sayings of the Desert Fathers*, 154.

Chapter 3 Preparation

1. *The Sayings of the Desert Fathers*, 93.

2. H. D. M. Spence and Joseph S. Exell, eds., *The Pulpit Commentary (Hebrews)* (Grand Rapids: Eerdmans, 1971), 139.

3. Ibid., 114.

4. Dina Spector, "Here's How Many Days a Person Can Survive Without Water," *Business Insider*, May 9, 2014, http://www.businessinsider.com/how
-many-days-can-you-survive-without-water-2014-5.

5. *The Sayings of the Desert Fathers*, 230.

Chapter 4 Provision

1. *The Sayings of the Desert Fathers*, 91.

2. Ibid., 43–44.

Chapter 5 Perspective

1. *The Sayings of the Desert Fathers*, 84.

2. Peter Billingham, "5 TED Talks on Death and Dying You Must Watch," *Death Goes Digital* (blog), February 19, 2016, http://www.deathgoesdigital.com
/blog/2016/5-ted-talks-on-death-and-dying.

3. www.google.com/search?q=define+perspective&ie=utf-8&oe=utf-8&
client=firefox-b-1.

4. *The Sayings of the Desert Fathers*, 63.

5. Ibid., 15.

Chapter 6 Rest

1. *The Sayings of the Desert Fathers*, 19.

2. H. D. M. Spence and Joseph S. Exell, eds., *The Pulpit Commentary (I and II Kings)* (Grand Rapids: Eerdmans, 1978), 458–59.

3. Kirsten Weir, "The Lasting Impact of Neglect," American Psychological Association, June 2014, http://www.apa.org/monitor/2014/06/neglect.aspx.

4. "Care for the Premature Baby," American Pregnancy Association, last updated April 12, 2017, http://americanpregnancy.org/labor-and
-birth/premature-care/; and Elsevier, "Loving Touch Critical for Premature

Infants," *Science Daily*, January 6, 2014, https://www.sciencedaily.com/releases /2014/01/140106094437.htm.

5. Spence and Exell, eds., 459.

6. "AAA Study Finds Risks of Drowsy Driving Comparable to Drunk Driving," CBS This Morning, December 6, 2016, http://www.cbsnews.com/news /aaa-study-drowsy-driving-dangers-comparable-to-drunk-driving/.

7. https://www.google.com/search?q=exhaust+etymology&ie=utf-8&oe =utf-8&client=firefox-b-1, accessed February 1, 2018.

8. *The Sayings of the Desert Fathers*, 92.

Chapter 7 Revelation

1. *The Sayings of the Desert Fathers*, 181.

2. ESV Study Bible (Wheaton: Crossway, 2008), 636.

3. "Splagchnizomai," Bible Hub, accessed February 1, 2018, http://bible hub.com/greek/4697.htm.

4. *The Sayings of the Desert Fathers*, 175.

Chapter 8 Intimacy

1. *The Sayings of the Desert Fathers*, 35.

2. Oxford NIV Scofield Study Bible, 894.

3. Howard F. Vos, *Nelson's New Illustrated Bible Manners and Customs* (Nashville: Thomas Nelson, 1999), 182–83.

4. ESV Study Bible (Wheaton: Crossway, 2008), 1620–21.

5. Vos, 115–16.

6. ESV Study Bible, 1626.

7. H. D. M. Spence and Joseph Exell, eds., *The Pulpit Commentary (Deuteronomy, Joshua and Judges)* (Grand Rapids: Eerdmans, 1978), 113.

8. Ibid., 119.

9. "Philos," Bible Hub, accessed February 1, 2018, http://biblehub.com /greek/5384.htm.

10. *The Sayings of the Desert Fathers*, 55.

Chapter 9 Solitude

1. *The Sayings of the Desert Fathers*, 140.

2. Ibid., 171.

3. Ibid., 22.

4. "Lonely," Online Etymology Dictionary, accessed February 1, 2018, https://www.etymonline.com/search?q=lonely.

5. "Solitude," https://www.etymonline.com/word/solitude.

6. H. D. M. Spence and Joseph S. Exell, eds., *The Pulpit Commentary (Exodus)* (Grand Rapids: Eerdmans, 1978), 37.

7. Ibid., 55.

8. Ibid.

9. *The Sayings of the Desert Fathers*, 220.

Chapter 10 Recognition

1. *The Sayings of the Desert Fathers*, 90.
2. Ibid., 27.
3. Hebrew OT Transliteration, Holy Name KJV, accessed February 1, 2018, http://www.qbible.com/hebrew-old-testament/genesis/16.html#6.
4. ESV Study Bible (Wheaton: Crossway, 2008), 78.
5. "Recognition," Oxford Living Dictionaries, accessed February 1, 2018, https://en.oxforddictionaries.com/definition/recognition.
6. Molly Soat, "Social Media Triggers a Dopamine High," *American Marketing Association*, accessed February 1, 2018, https://www.ama.org/publications /MarketingNews/Pages/feeding-the-addiction.aspx.
7. *The Sayings of the Desert Fathers*, 2.

Chapter 11 Strength

1. *The Sayings of the Desert Fathers*, 209.
2. ESV Study Bible (Wheaton: Crossway, 2008), 1012.
3. H. D. M. Spence and Joseph S. Exell, eds., *The Pulpit Commentary (Ruth, I and II Samuel)* (Grand Rapids: Eerdmans 1978), 376.
4. *The Sayings of the Desert Fathers*, 233.
5. Ibid., 231.

Chapter 12 Beauty and Bounty

1. *The Sayings of the Desert Fathers*, 113.
2. Rebecca Fineman, "An Overview of Israeli Wine," GuildSomm, June 10, 2016, https://www.guildsomm.com/public_content/features/features /b/rebecca_fineman/posts/an-overview-of-israeli-wine.
3. Ibid.
4. Dan Savery Raz, "The Negev Desert Wine Route," BBC, February 27, 2012, http://www.bbc.com/travel/story/20120226-the-negev-desert-wine-route.
5. Ibid.
6. Luiz, "How Does Soil Influence Wine Quality," *The Wine Hub*, November 13, 2015, http://thewinehub.com/home/2015/11/13/how-does-soil-influ ence-wine-quality/.
7. Julie Christensen, "How Long Do Grapevines Live?" *SFGate*, accessed February 1, 2018, http://homeguides.sfgate.com/long-grapevines-live-762 83.html.
8. Stacy Horn, "Singing Changes Your Brain," *Time*, August 16, 2013, http://ideas.time.com/2013/08/16/singing-changes-your-brain/.
9. Maxin Boon, "'Musical Neurons' Discovered in the Brain's Auditory Cortex," *Limelight*, December 22, 2015, https://www.limelightmagazine.com .au/news/musical-neurons-discovered-in-the-brains-auditory-cortex/.
10. Sarah Gibbens, "See One of Earth's Driest Places Experience Rare Flower Boom," *National Geographic*, August 30, 2017, http://news.nationalgeogr aphic.com/2017/08/chile-atacama-desert-wildflower-super-bloom-video-spd/.

Allison Allen is a graduate of the prestigious Carnegie Mellon University and appeared in approximately 650 performances of the Broadway production of *Grease*. A former Women of Faith dramatist and current Bible teacher, she speaks to women at conferences and retreats around the country, exploring themes of purpose, value, and identity in original and unexpected ways. She lives with her beloveds in Tennessee.

It's time you stepped into the **LIGHT** of

God's role for you.

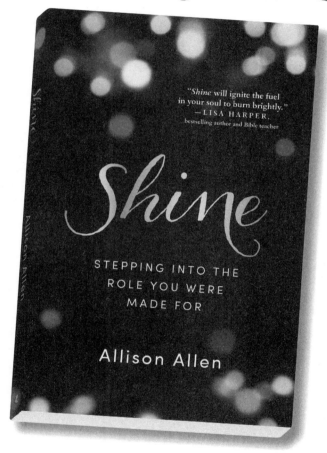

"The life-giving content on these pages has the power to fill your sails
with holy wind and literally change the trajectory of your story!"

—**LISA HARPER**, bestselling author and Bible teacher

 Revell
a division of Baker Publishing Group
www.RevellBooks.com

Available wherever books and ebooks are sold.